Funny Mom

QUOTES COLORING BOOK

Belongs to :

____

ENGINE
BOOK
MARKET
Best quality Low Content Books

COLOR TEST

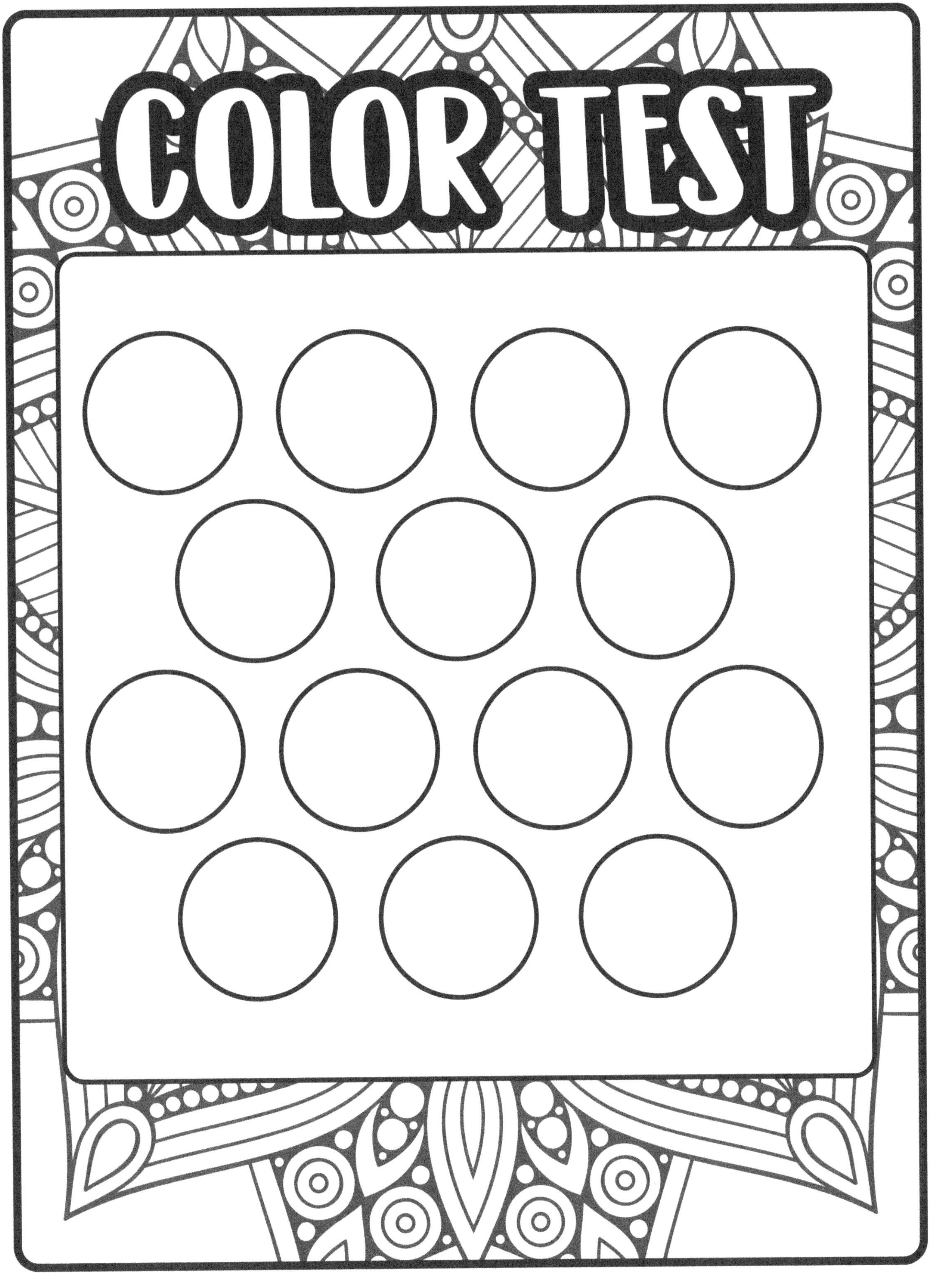

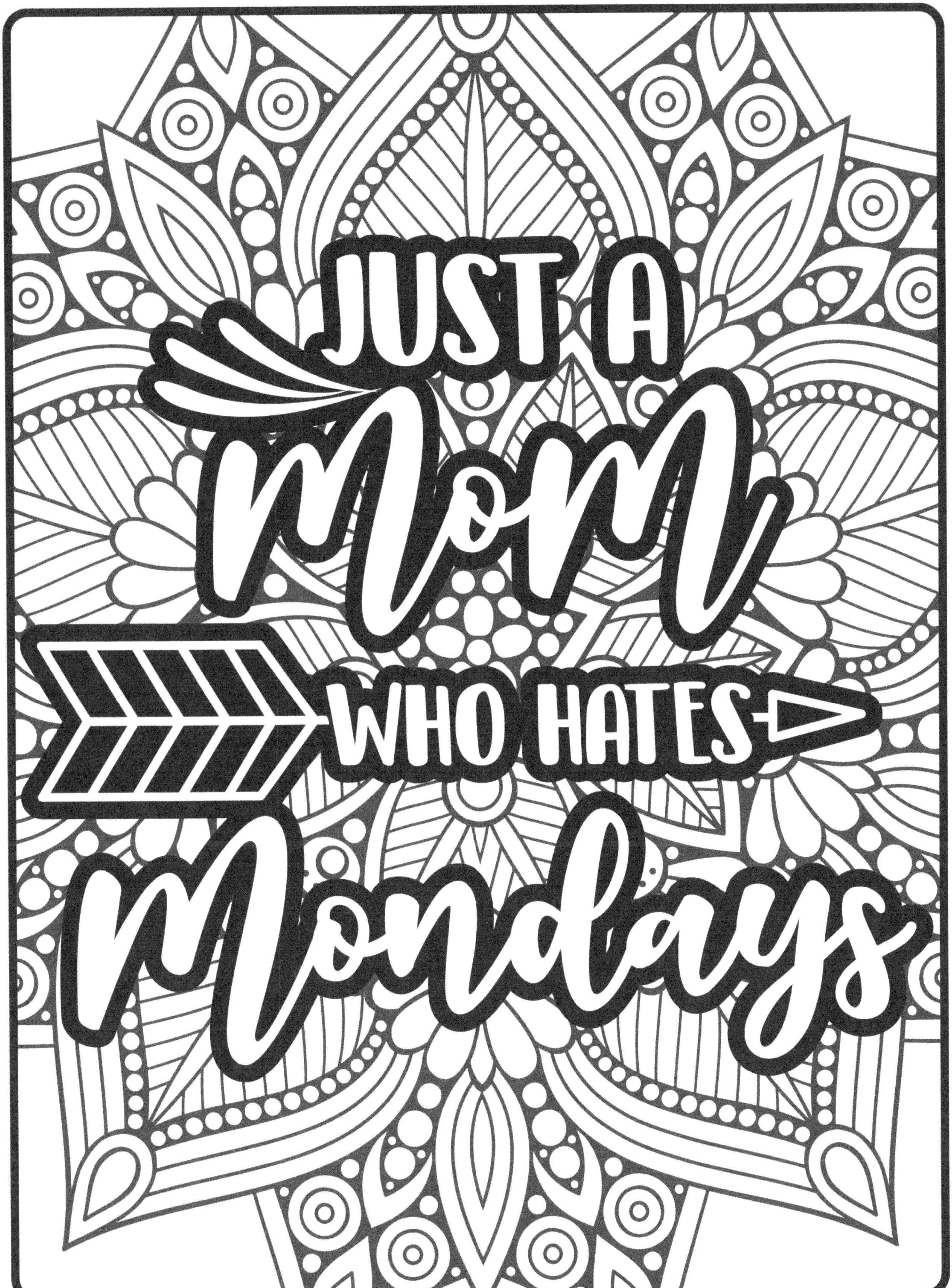
JUST A
Mom
WHO HATES
Mondays

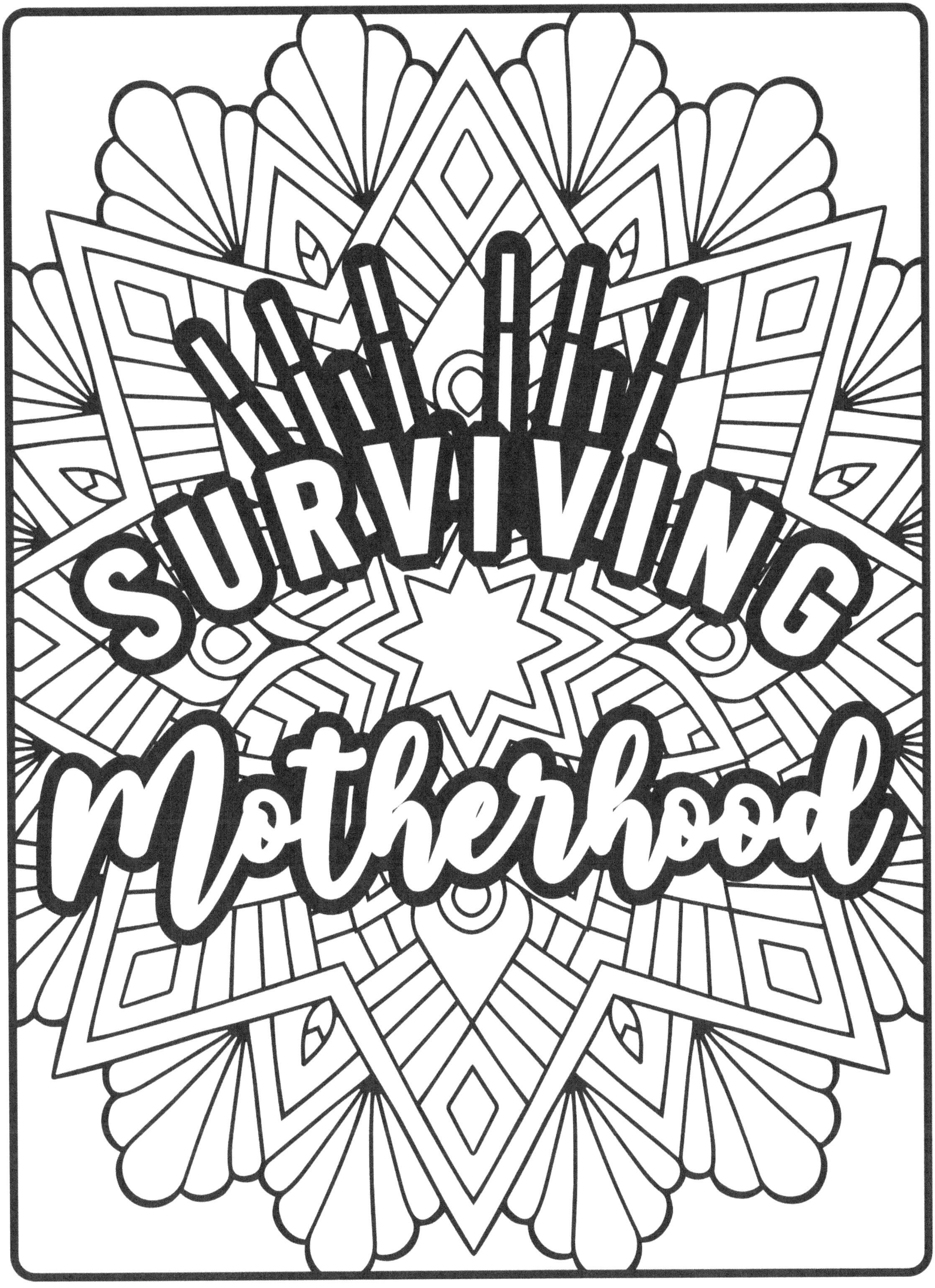
SURVIVING
Motherhood

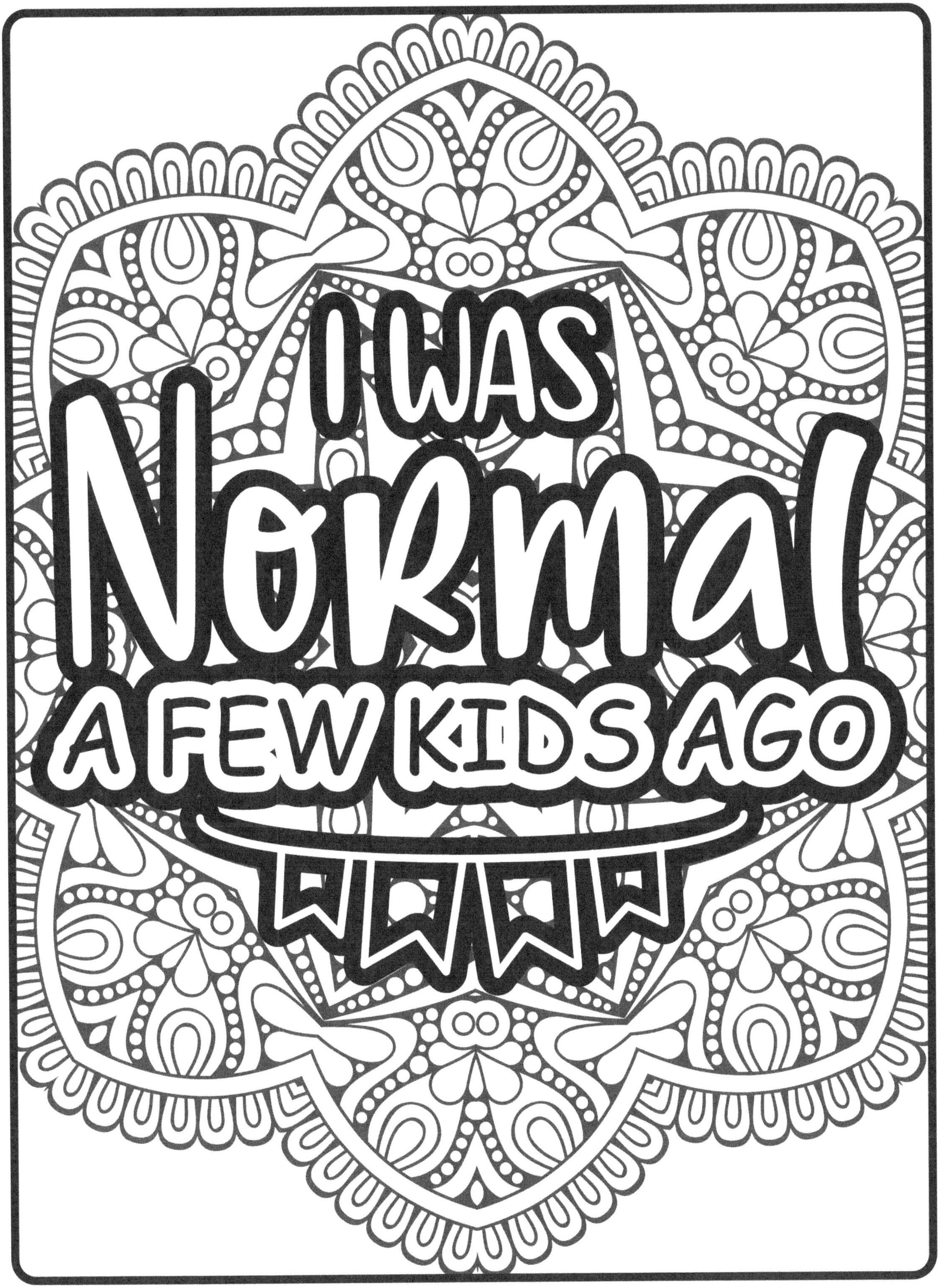
I WAS
Normal
A FEW KIDS AGO

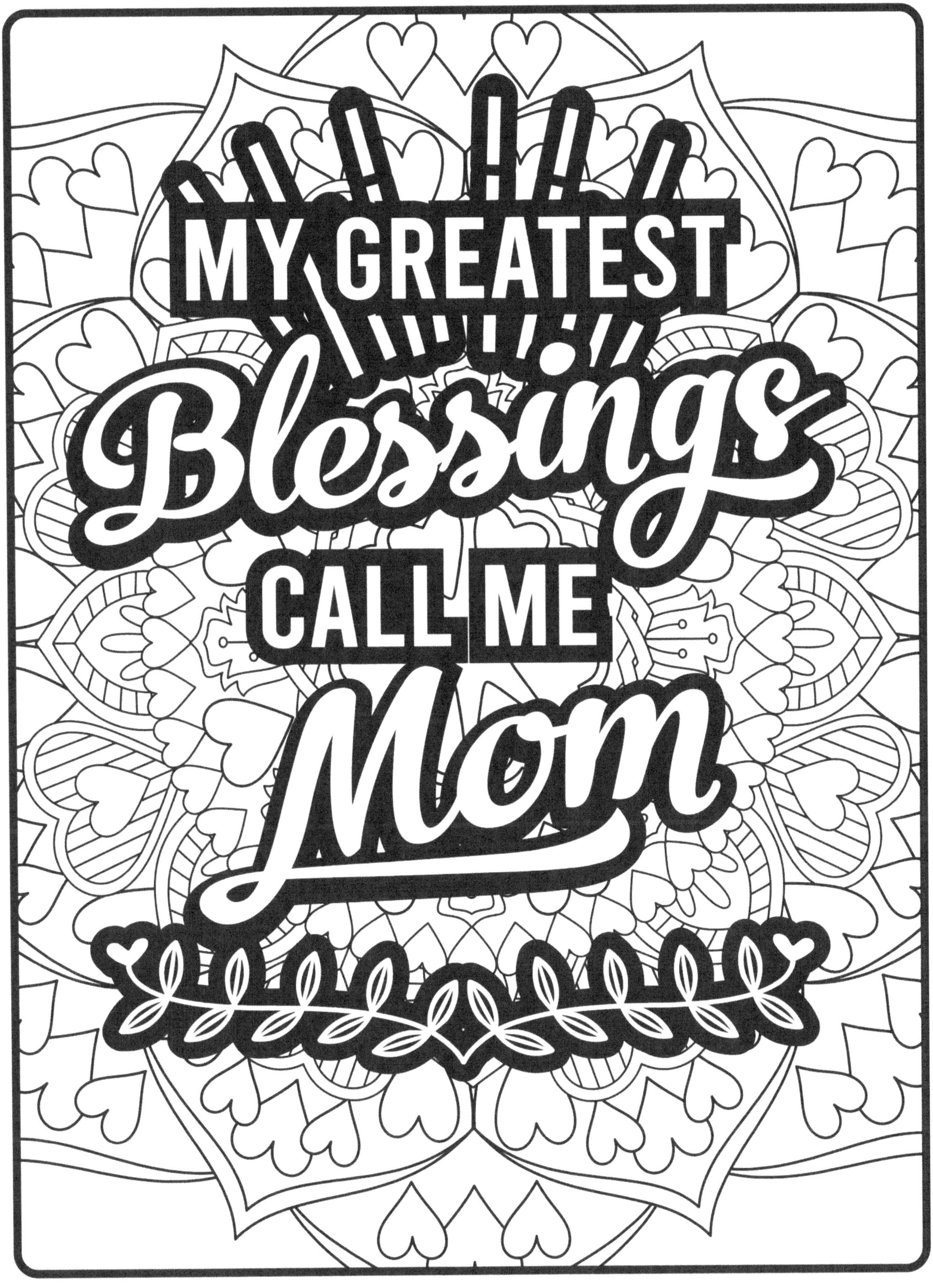
MY GREATEST
Blessings
CALL ME
Mom

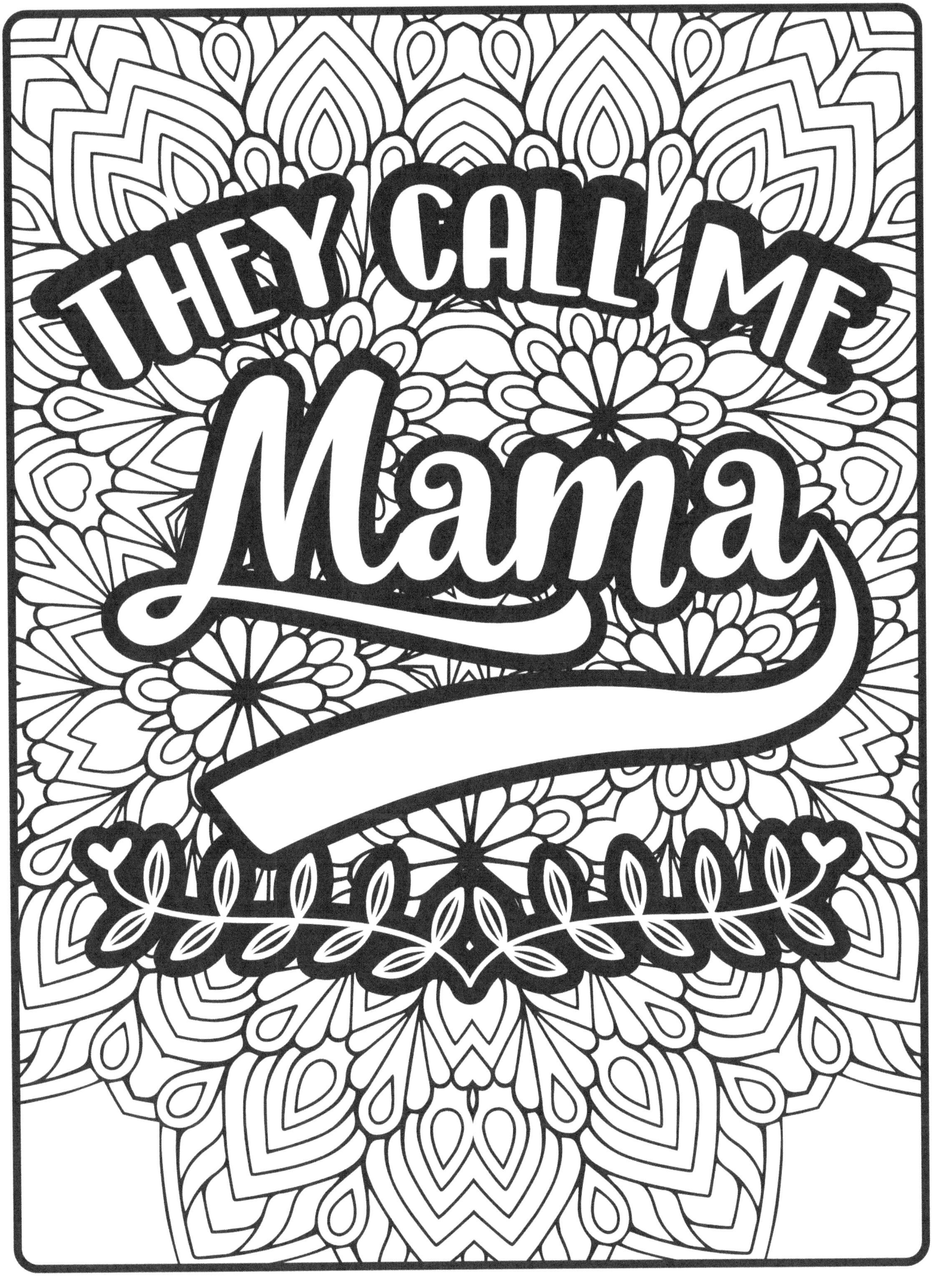
THEY CALL ME
Mama

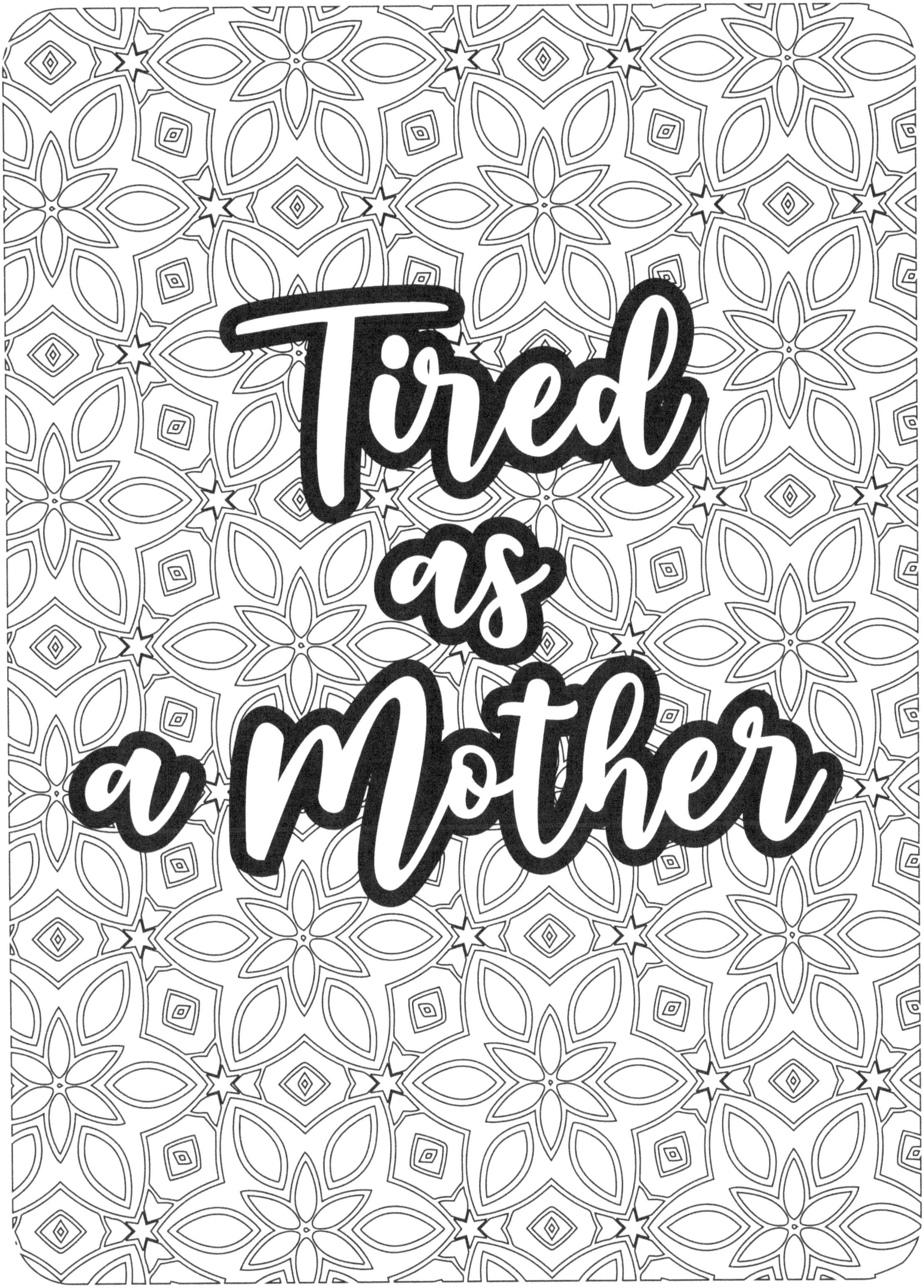
Tired
as
a Mother

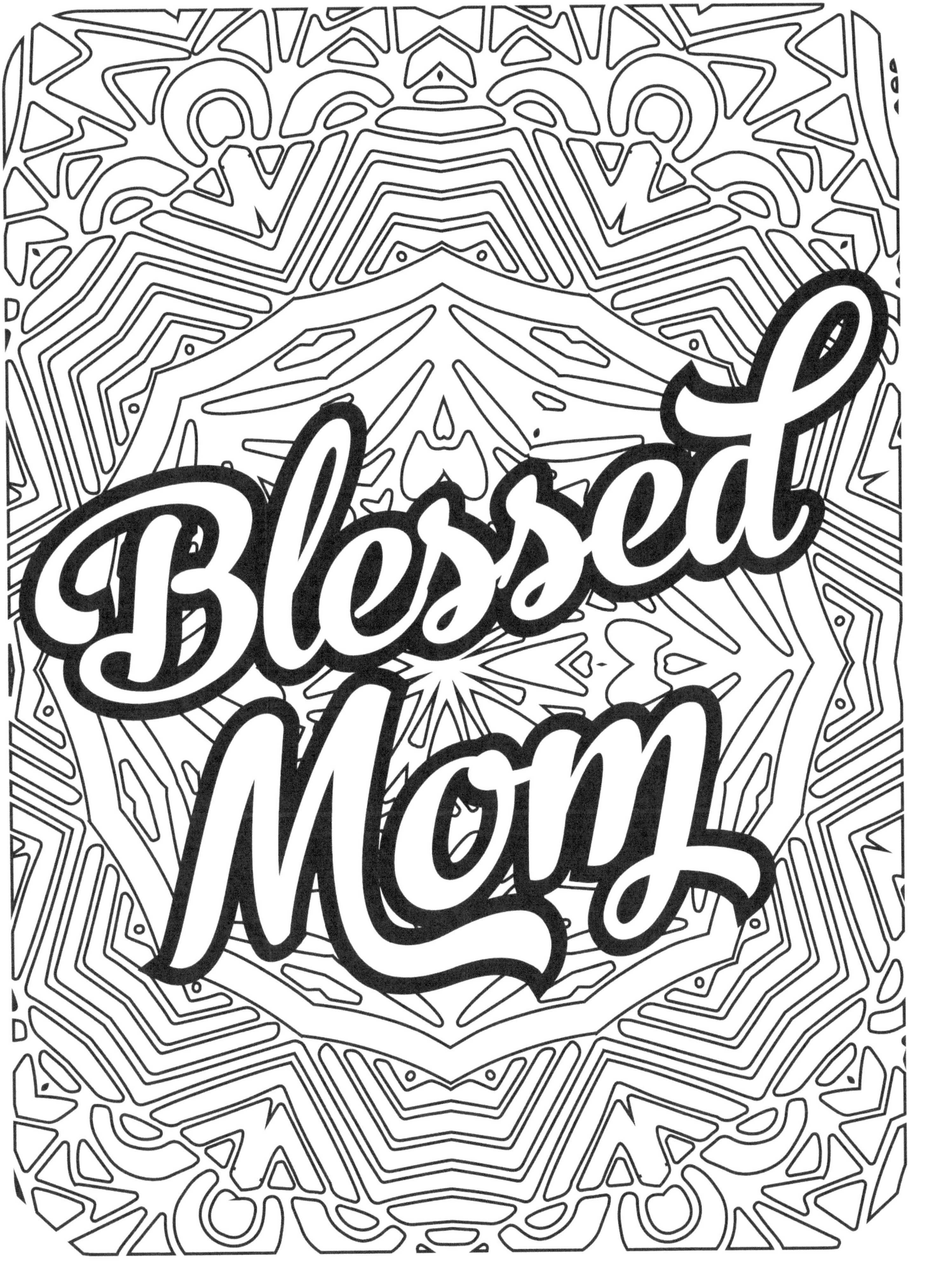
Blessed
Mom

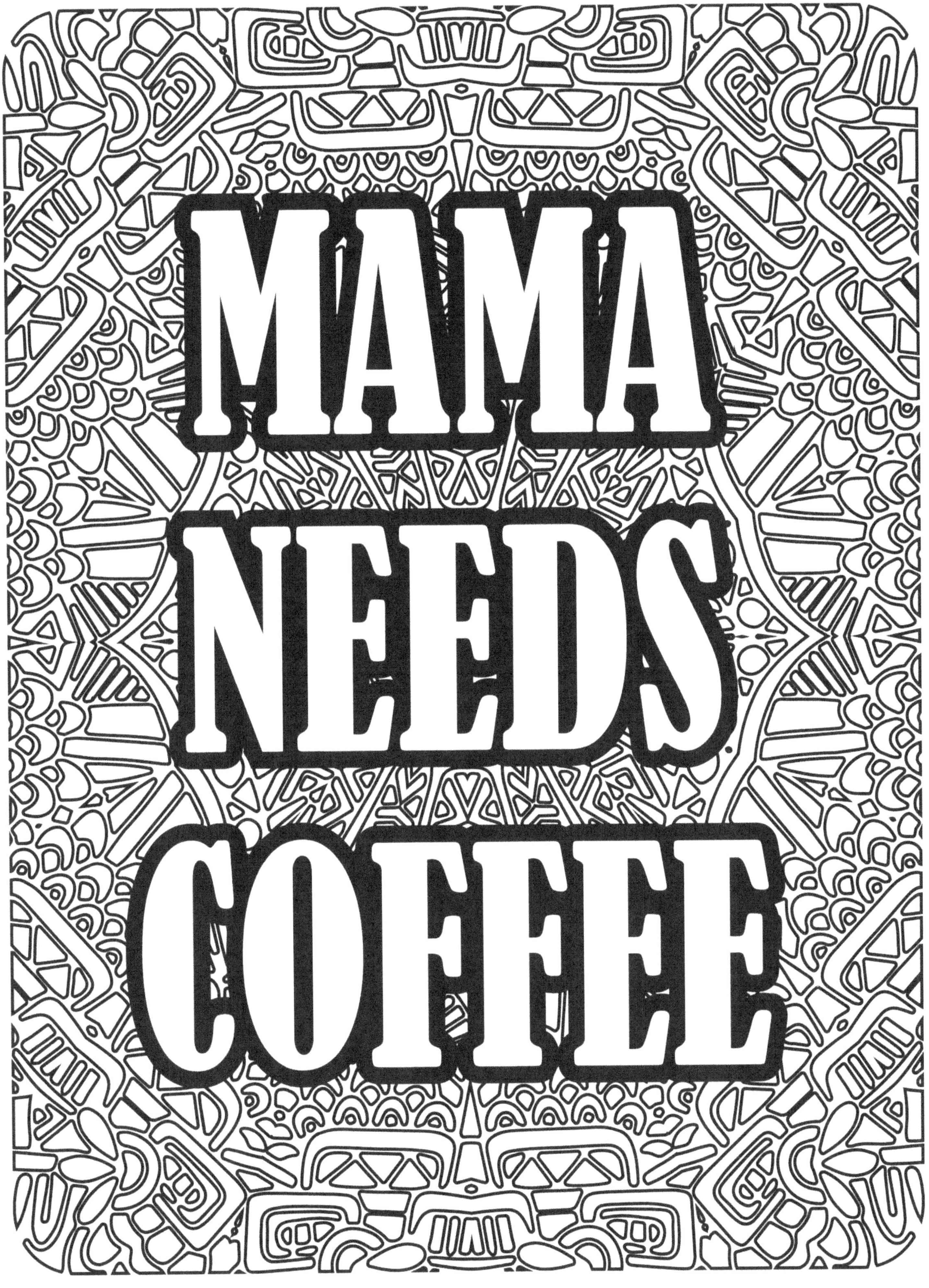
MAMA
NEEDS
COFFEE

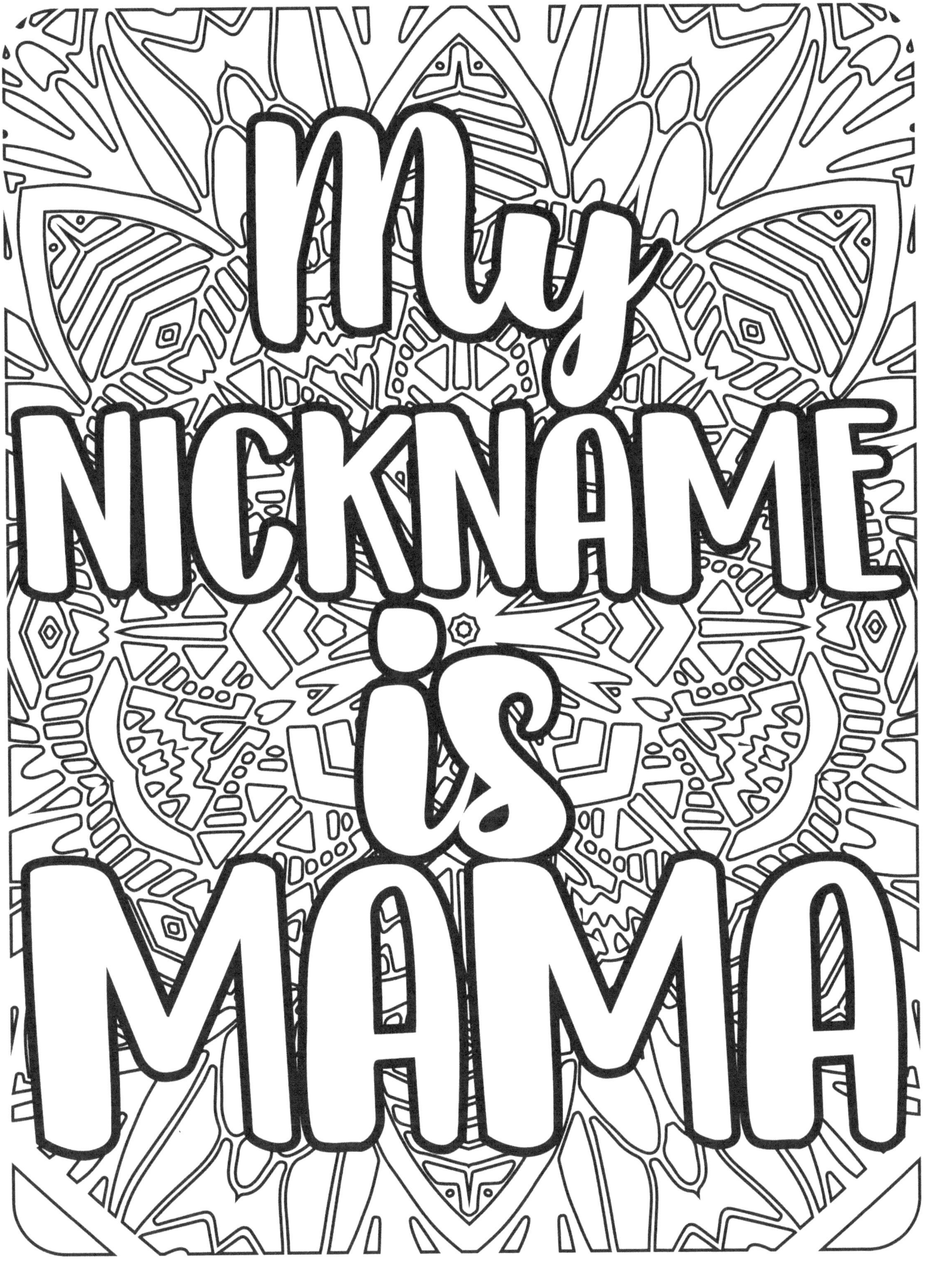
My
NICKNAME
is
MAMA

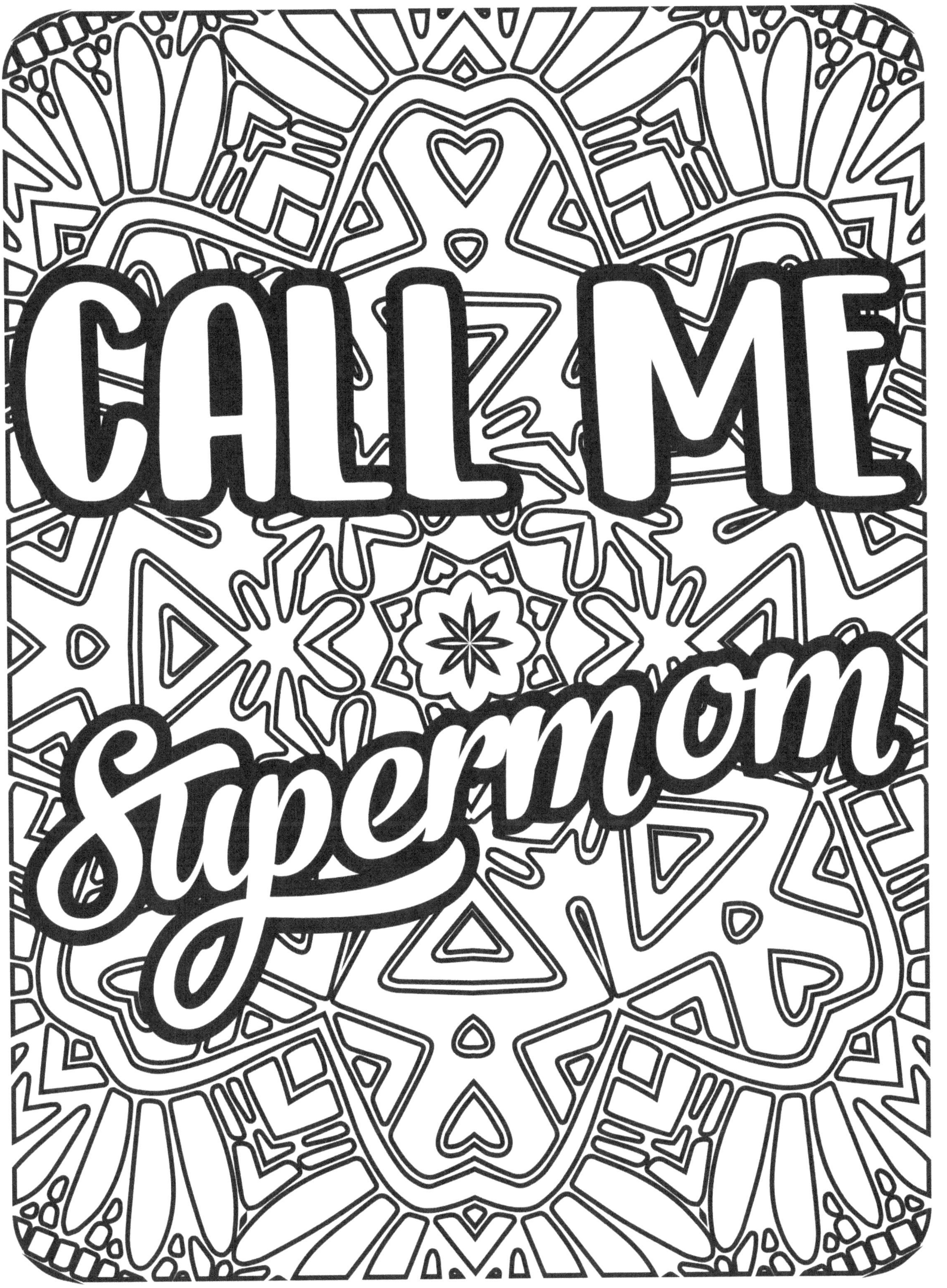
CALL ME
Supermom

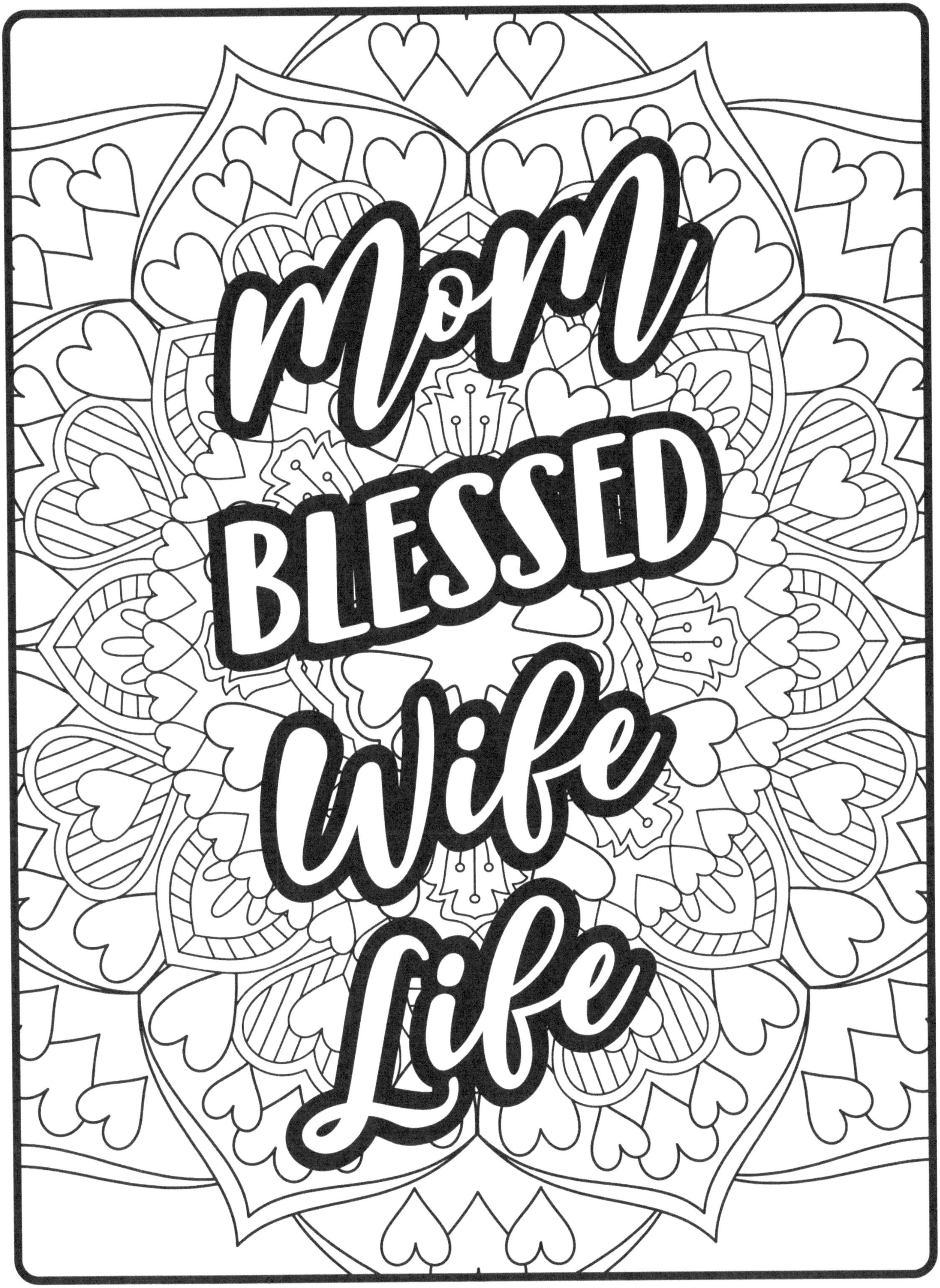
Mom
BLESSED
Wife
Life

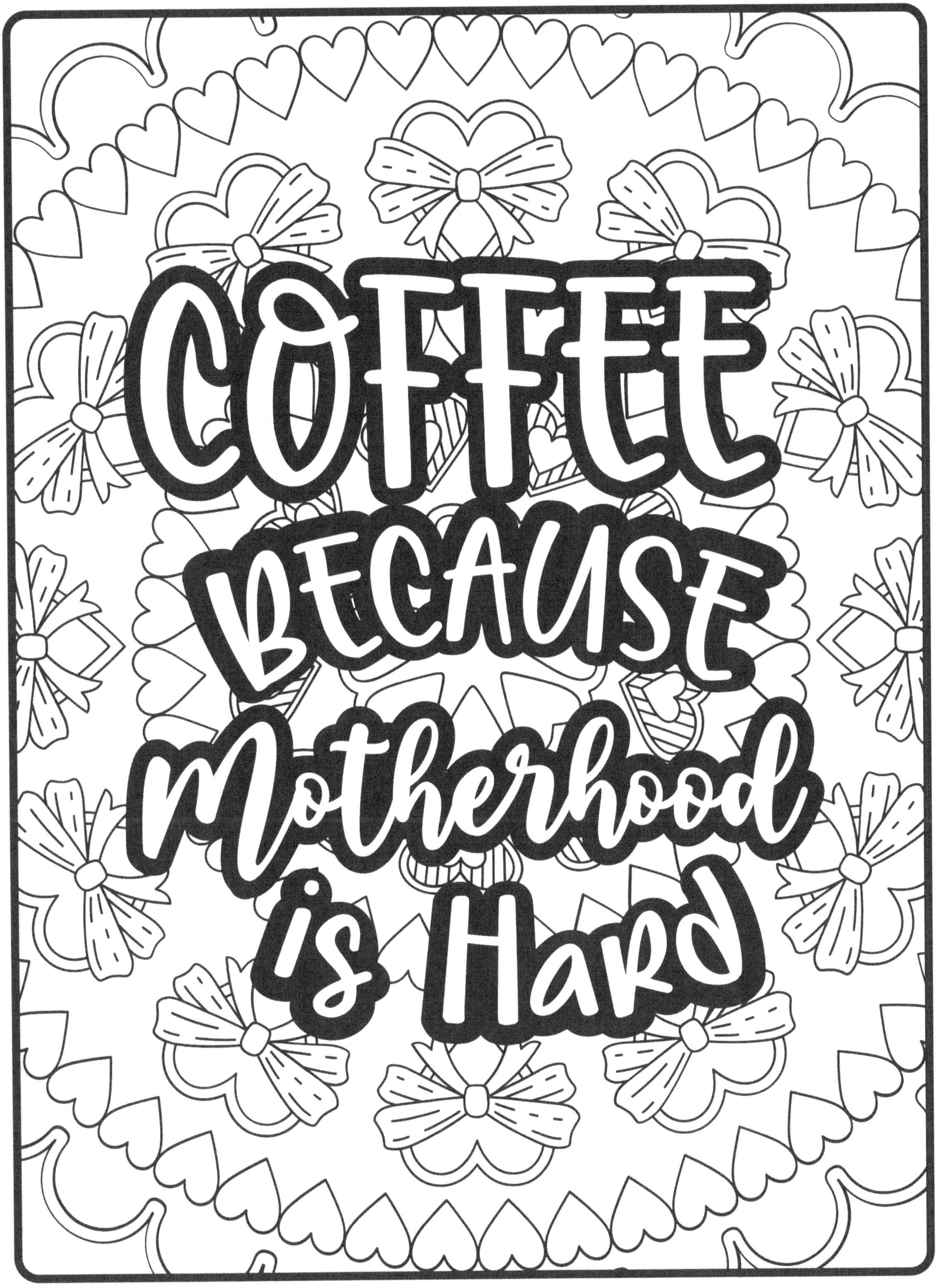
COFFEE
BECAUSE
Motherhood
is Hard

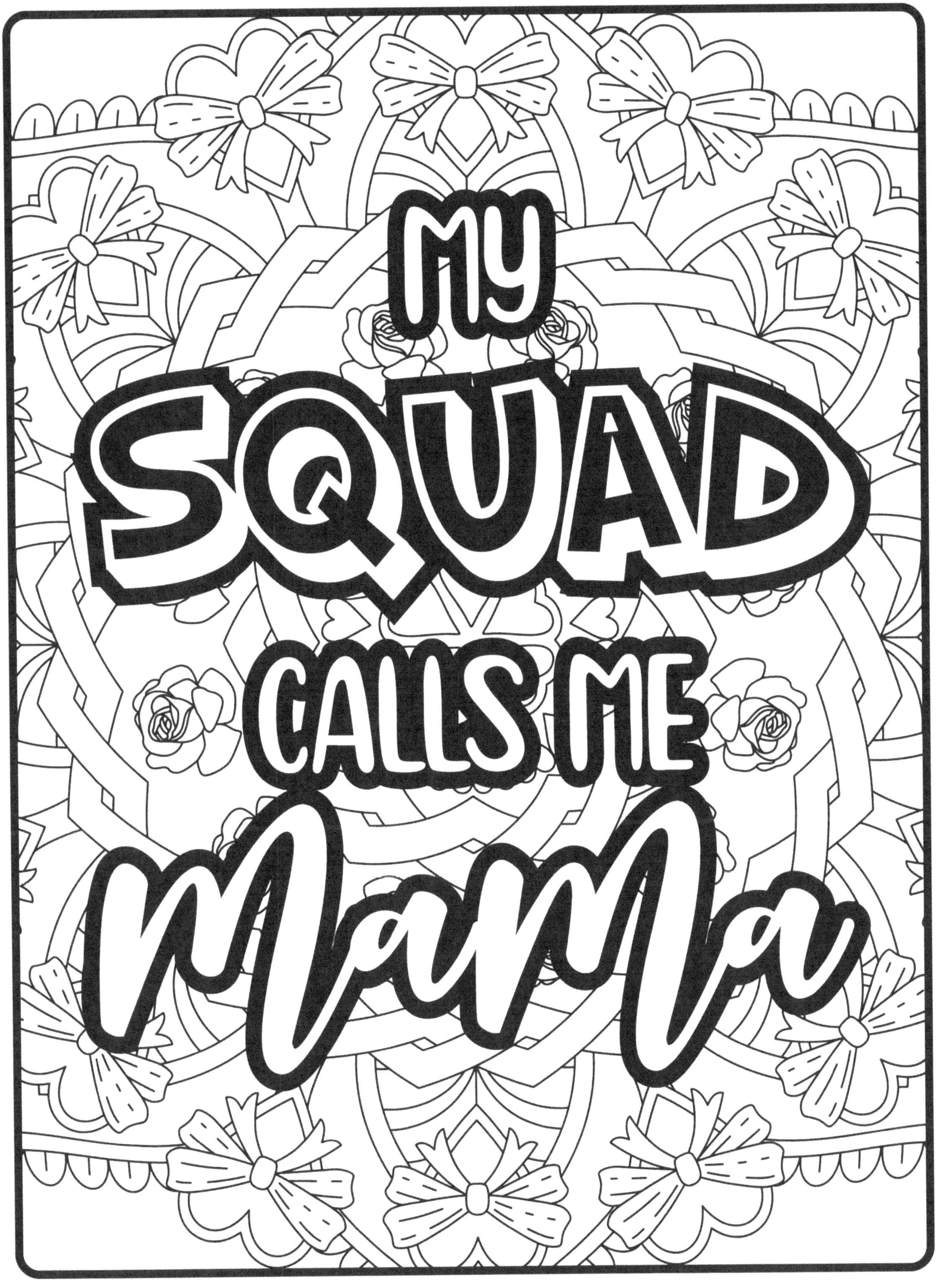
MY
SQUAD
CALLS ME
MaMa

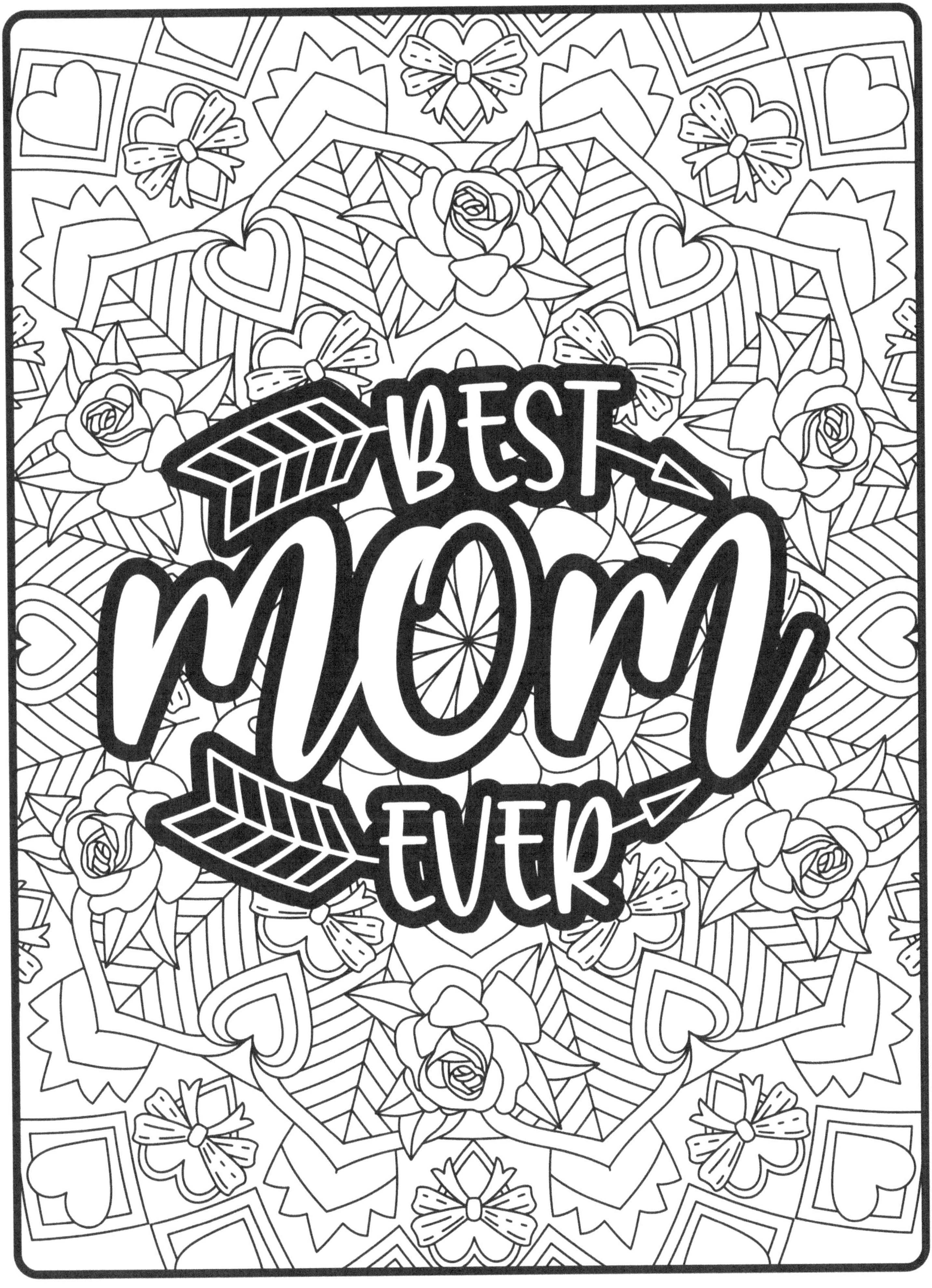
BEST
mom
EVER

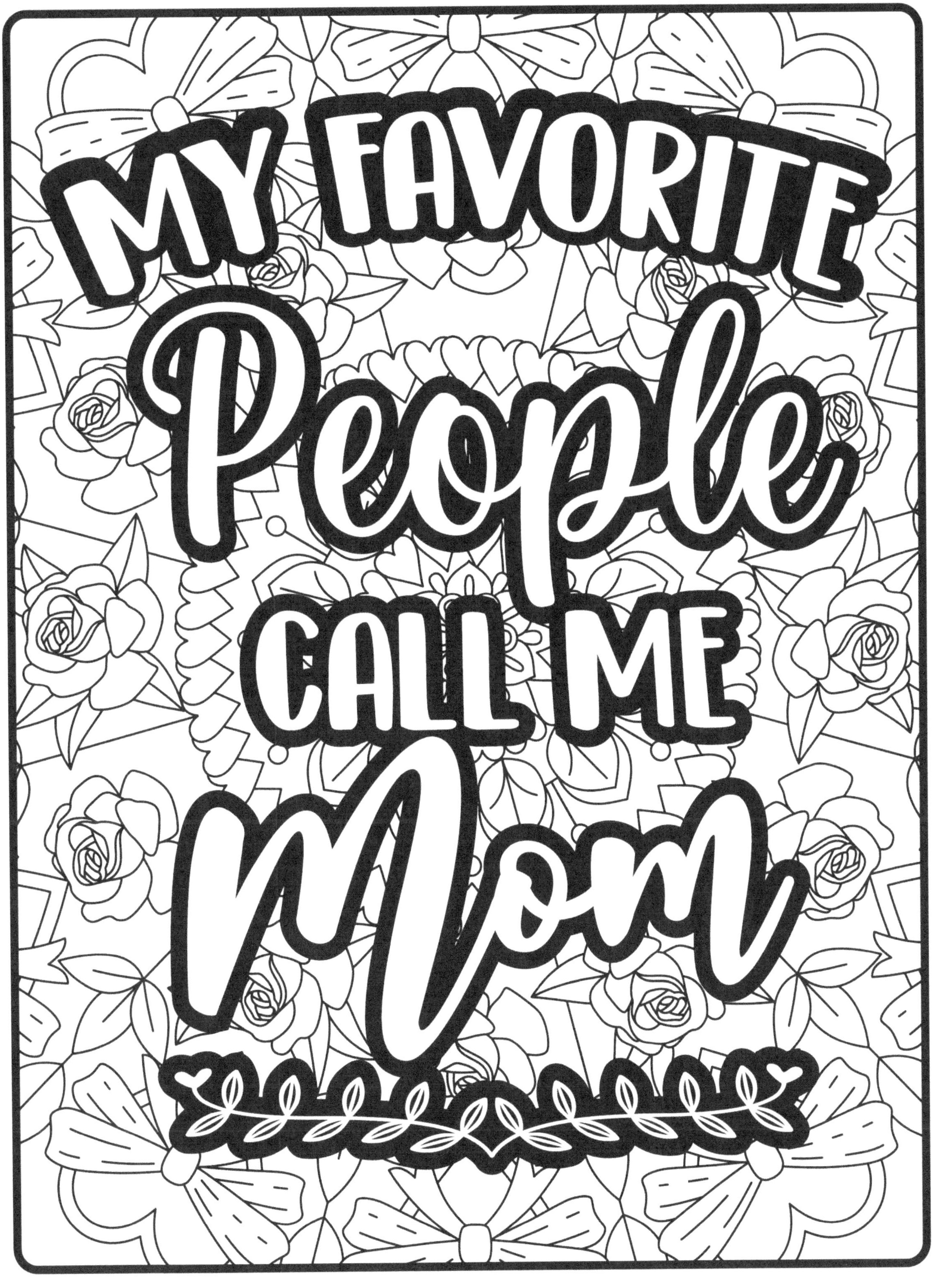
MY FAVORITE
People
CALL ME
Mom

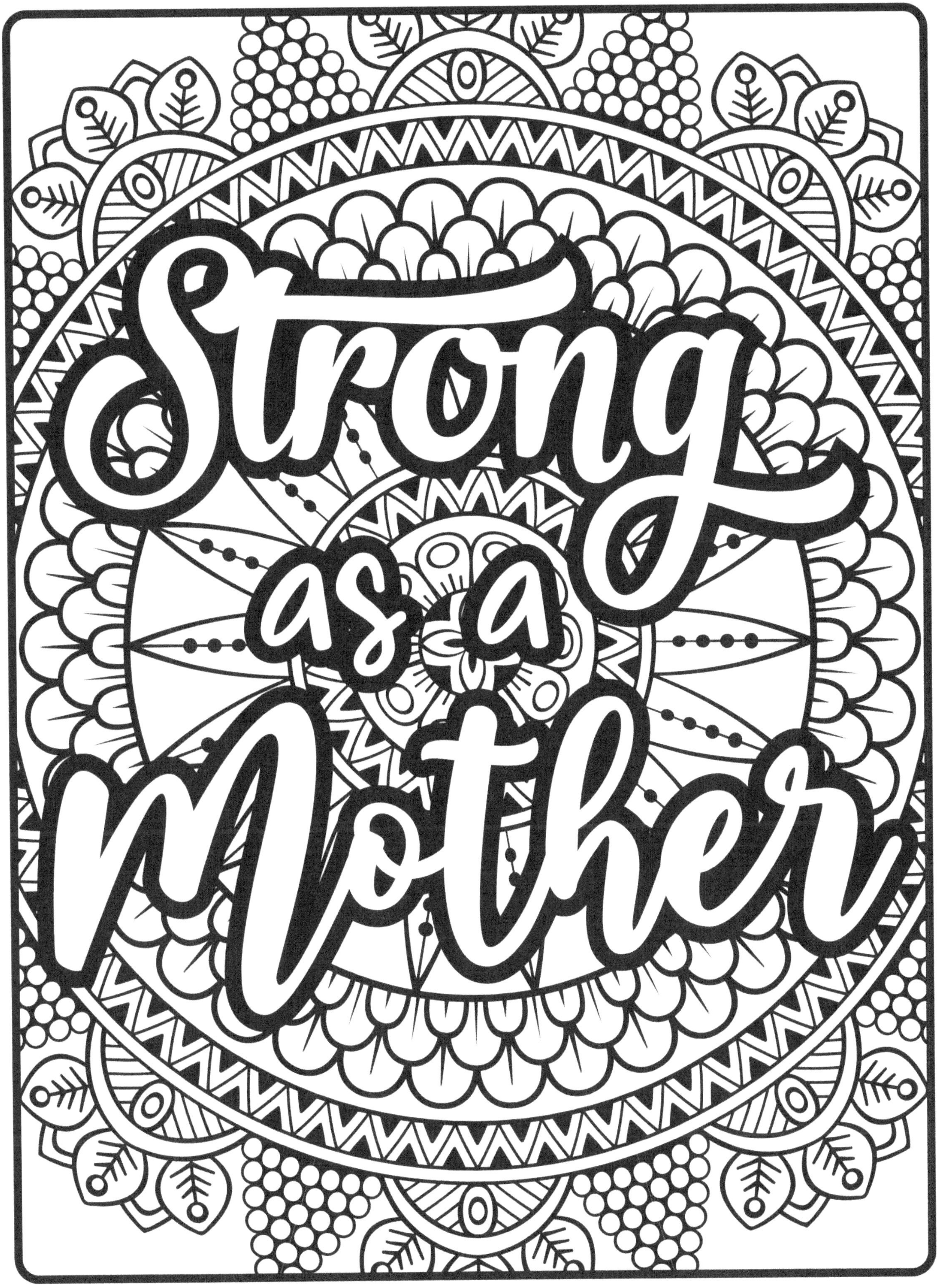
Strong
as a
Mother

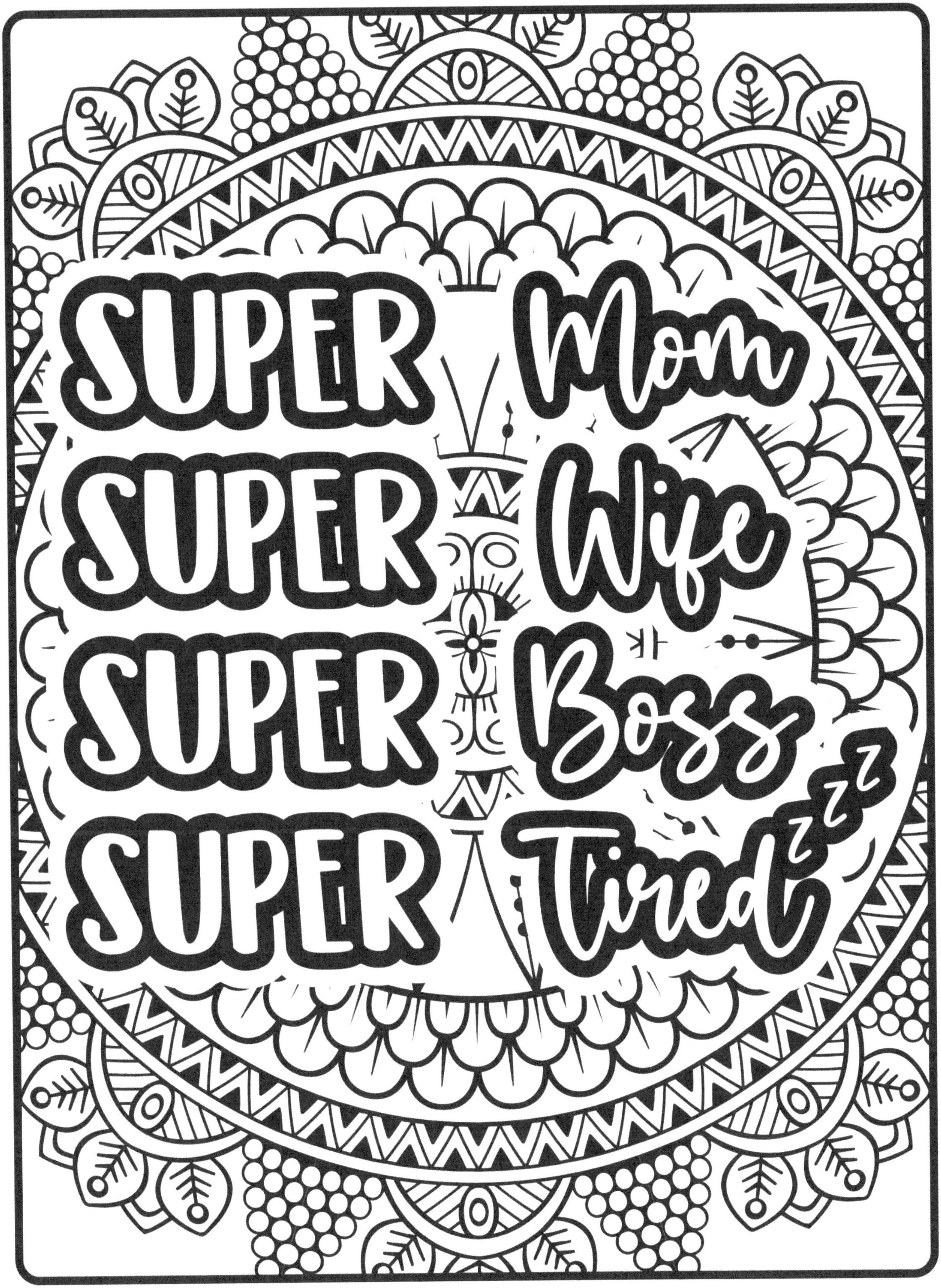
SUPER Mom
SUPER Wife
SUPER Boss
SUPER Tired zzz

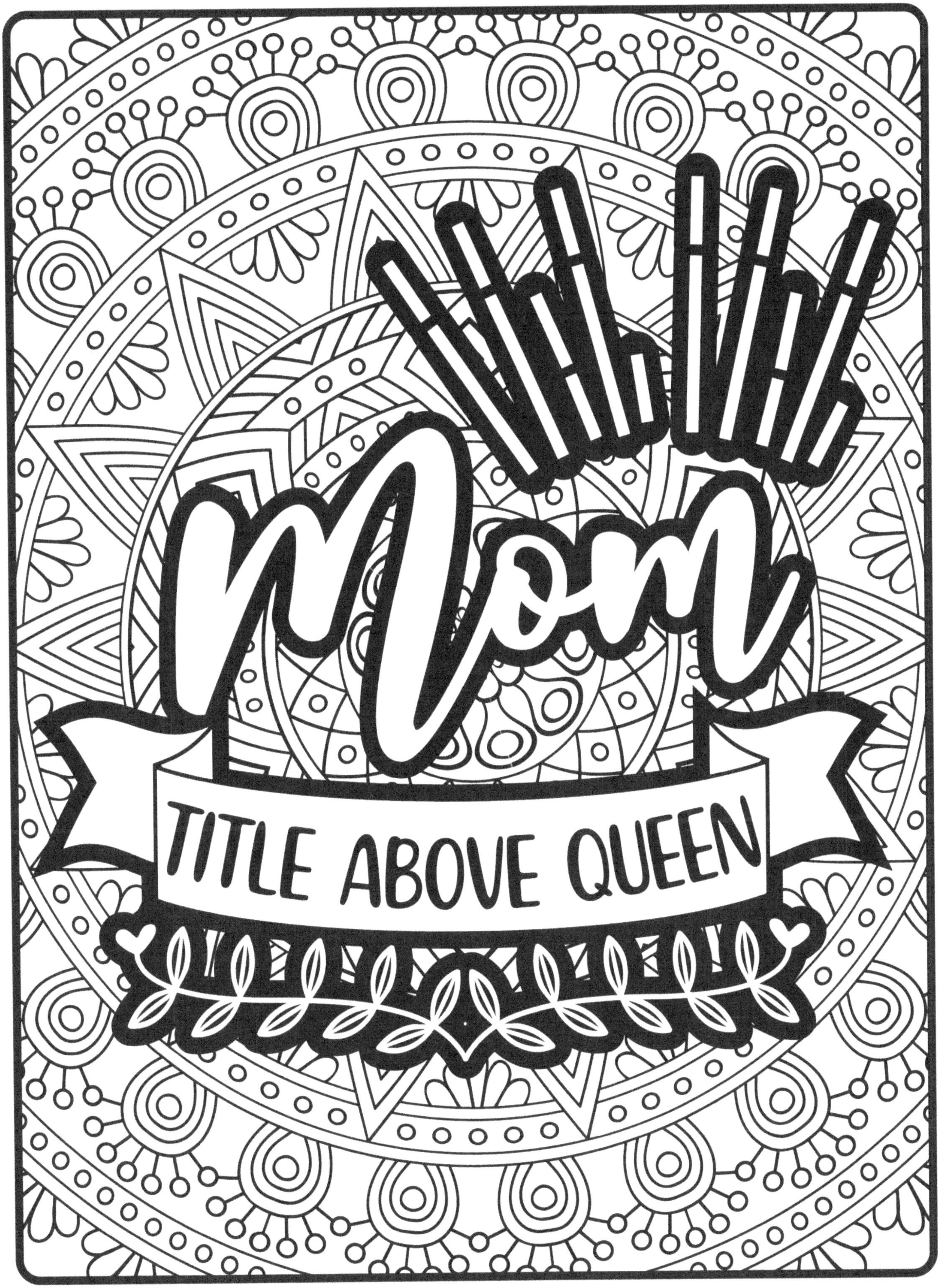
Mom
TITLE ABOVE QUEEN

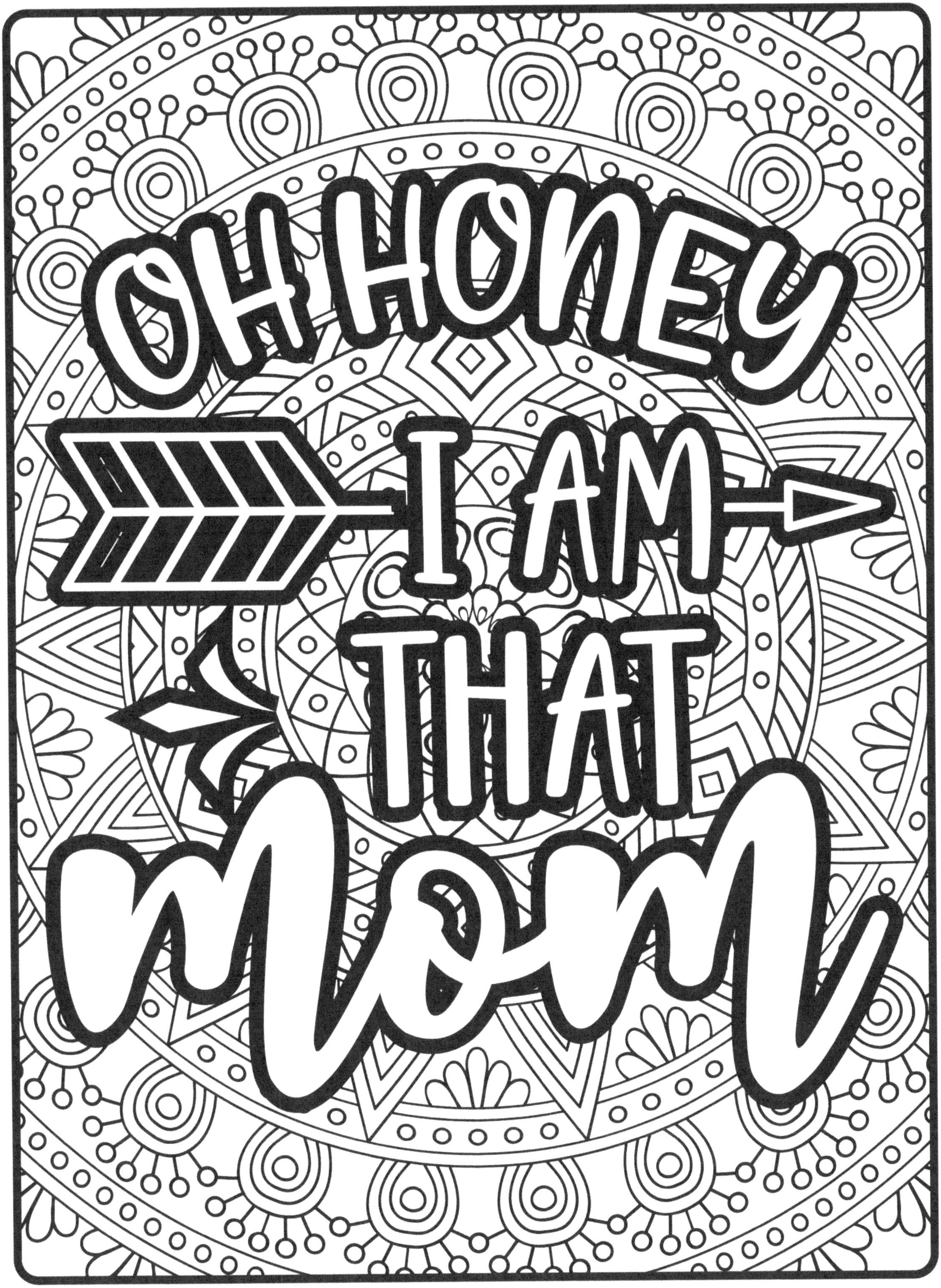
OH HONEY
I AM
THAT
mom

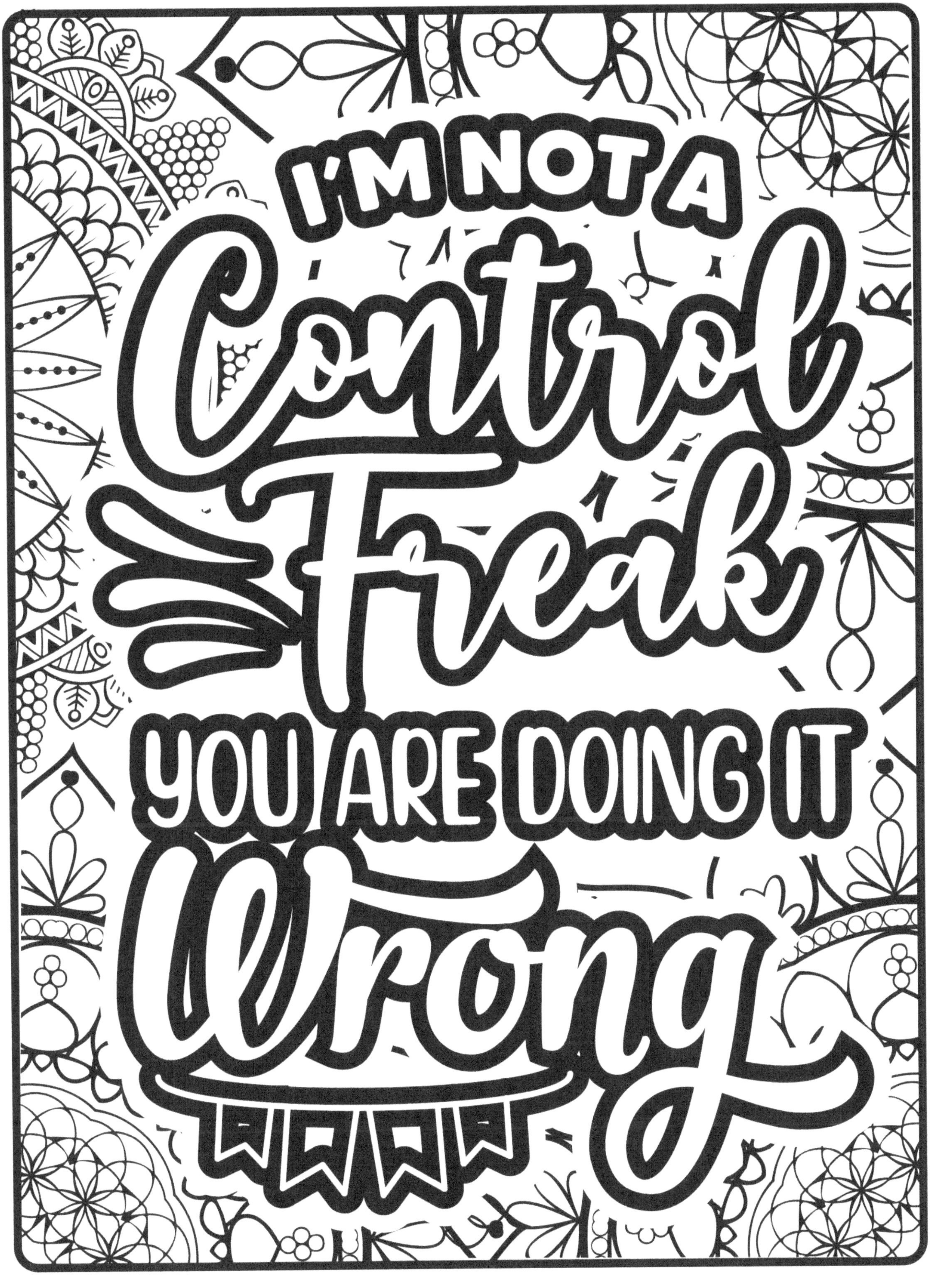
I'M NOT A
Control
Freak
YOU ARE DOING IT
Wrong

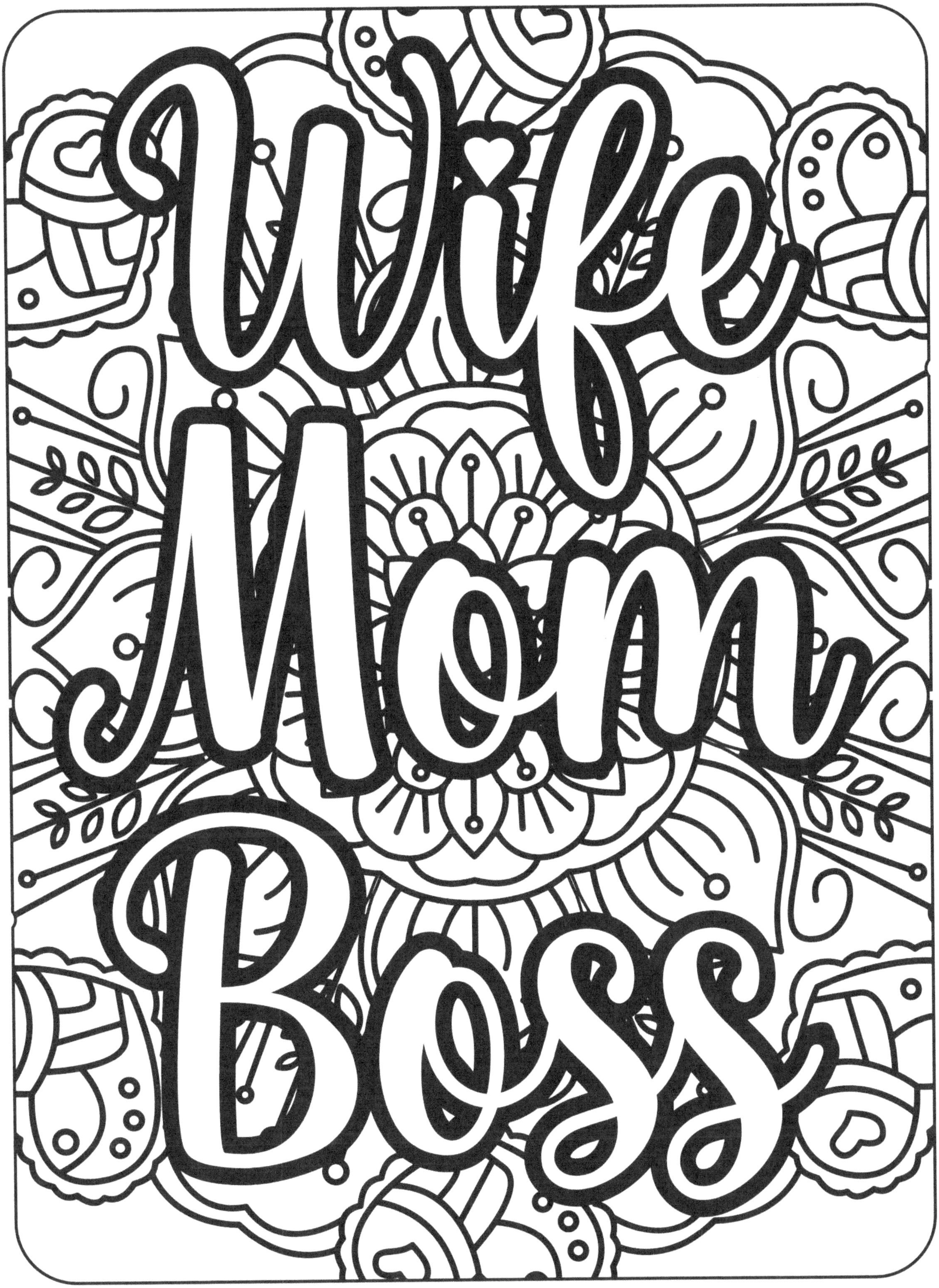
Wife
Mom
Boss

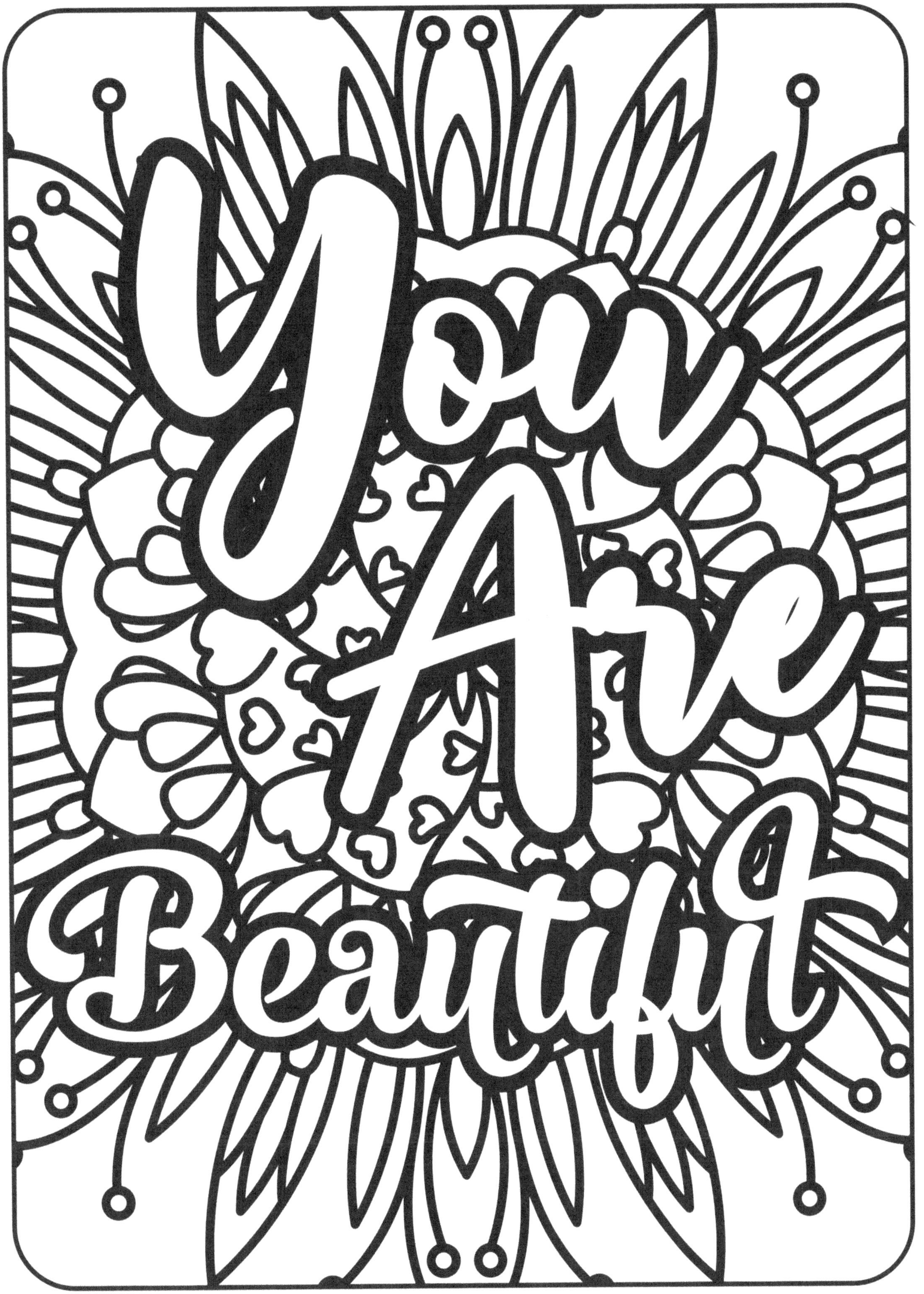
You Are Beautiful

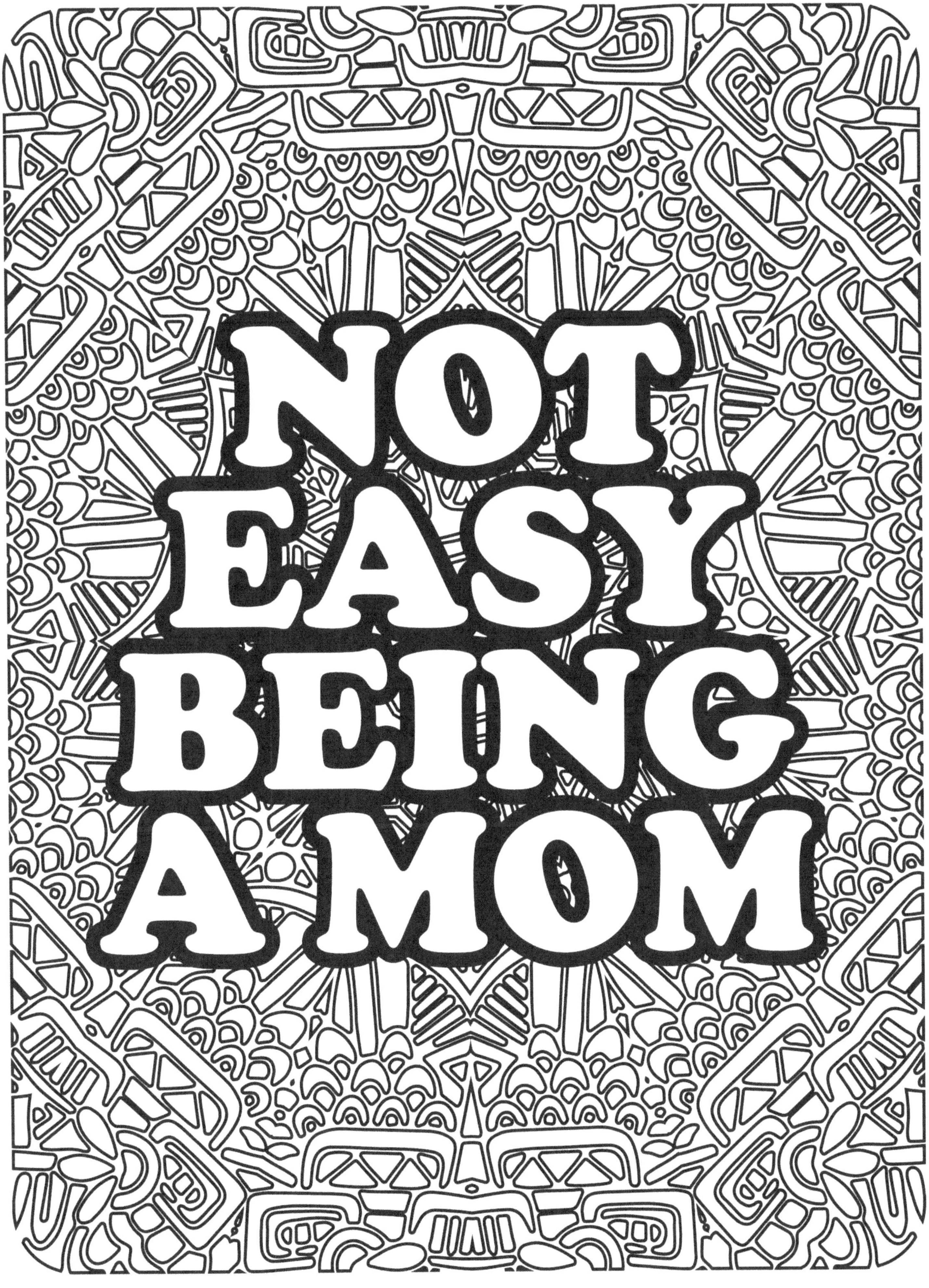
NOT
EASY
BEING
A MOM

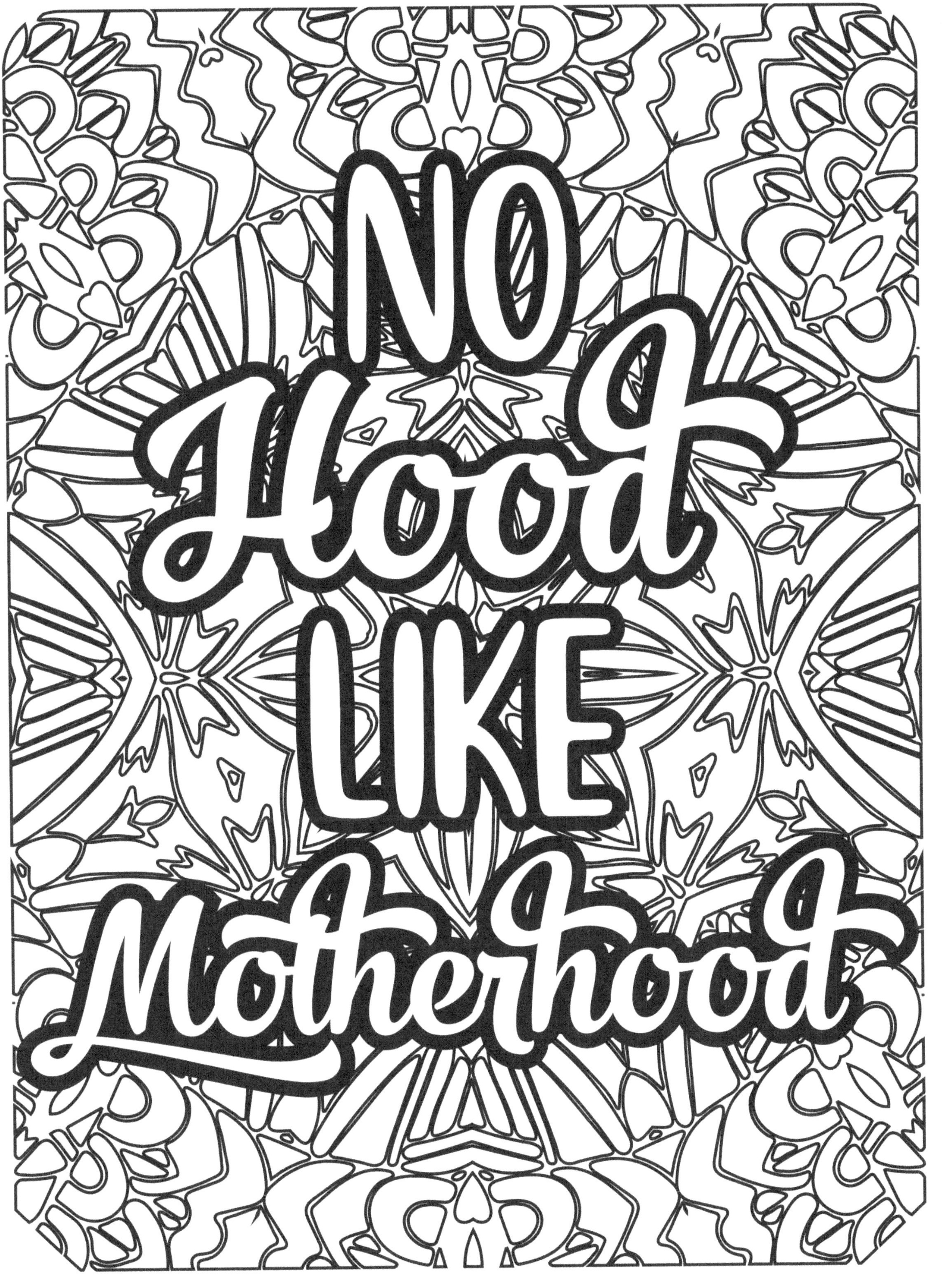
NO
Hood
LIKE
Motherhood

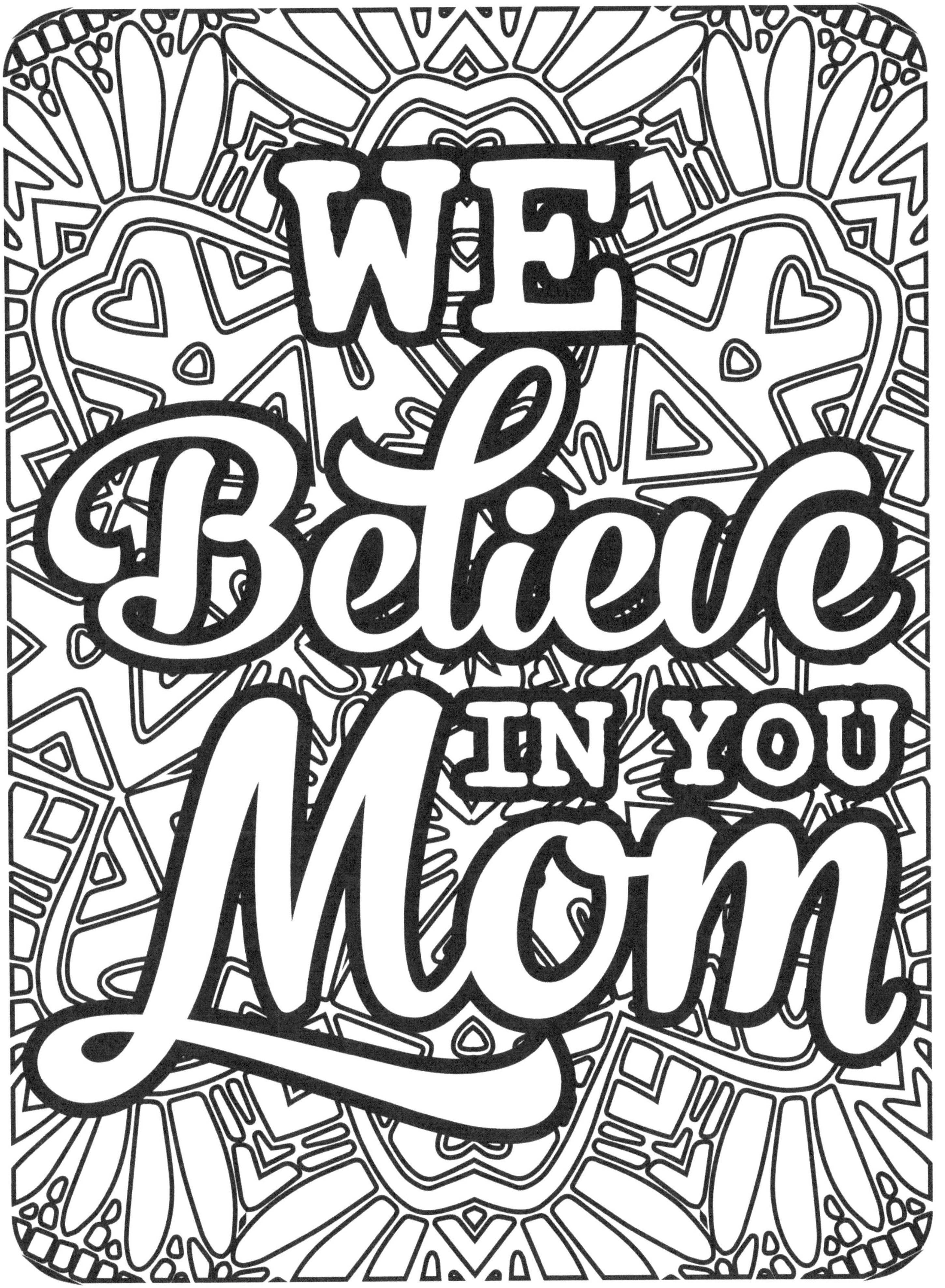
WE
Believe
IN YOU
Mom

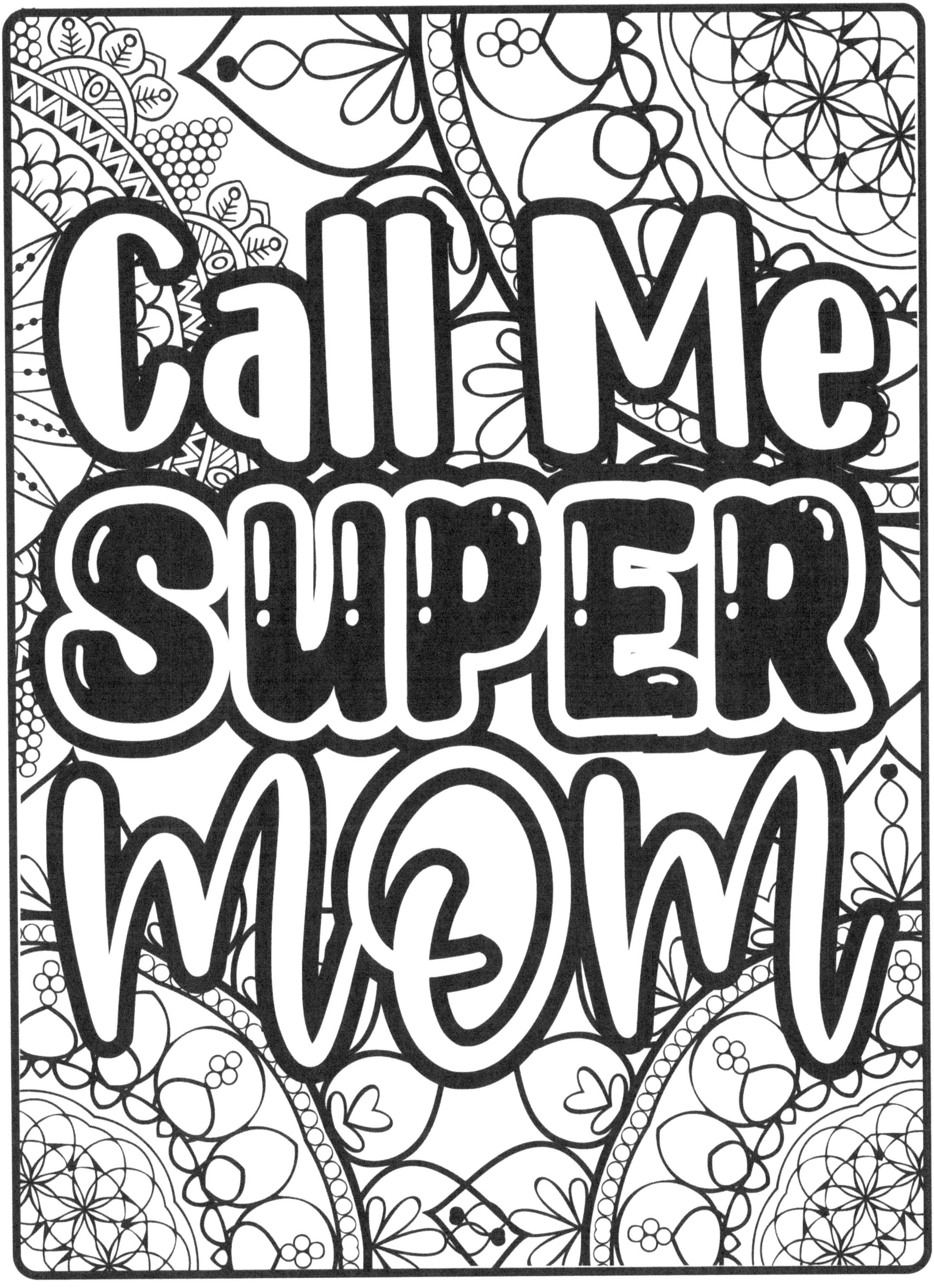
Call Me
SUPER
MOM

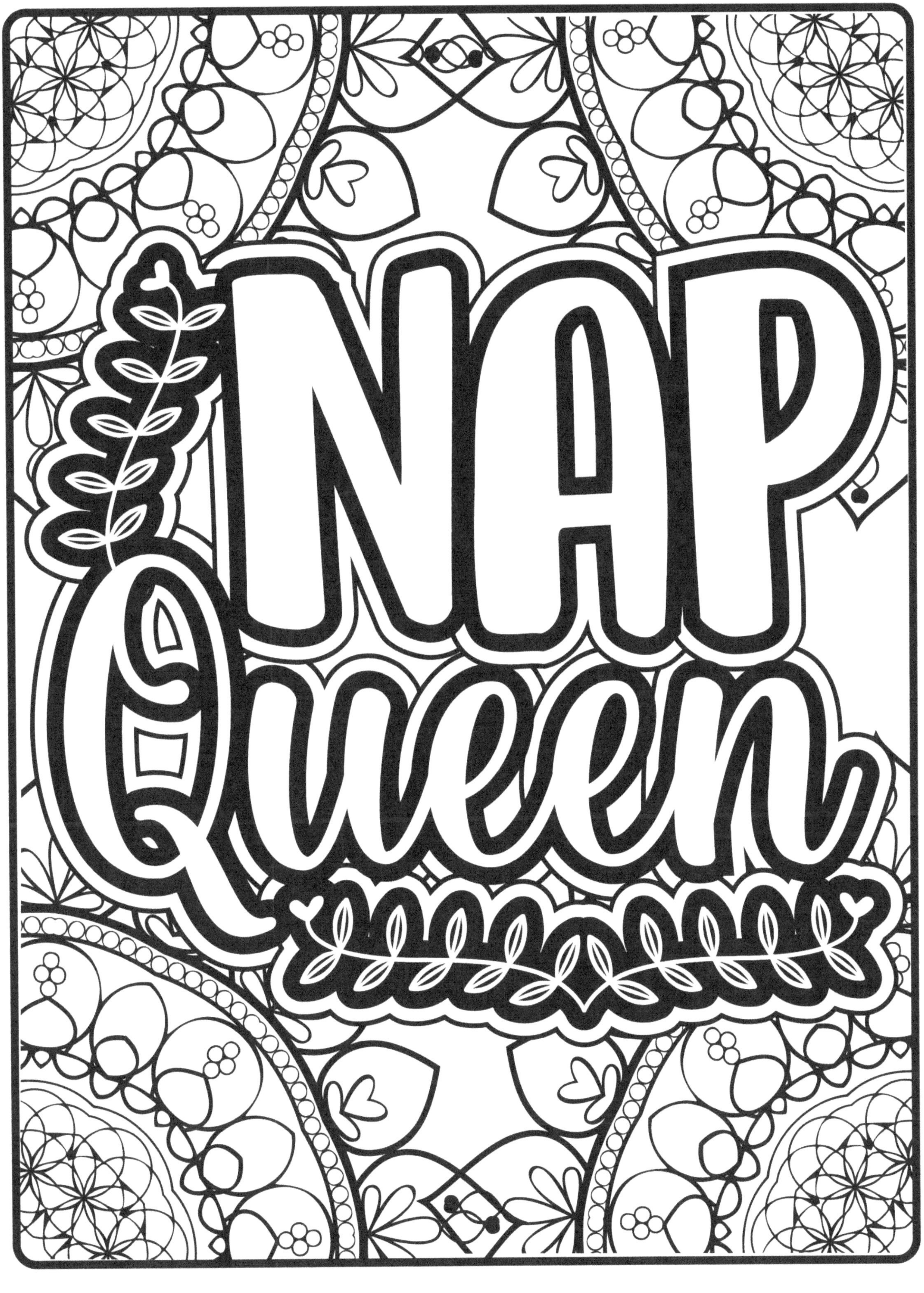
NAP
Queen

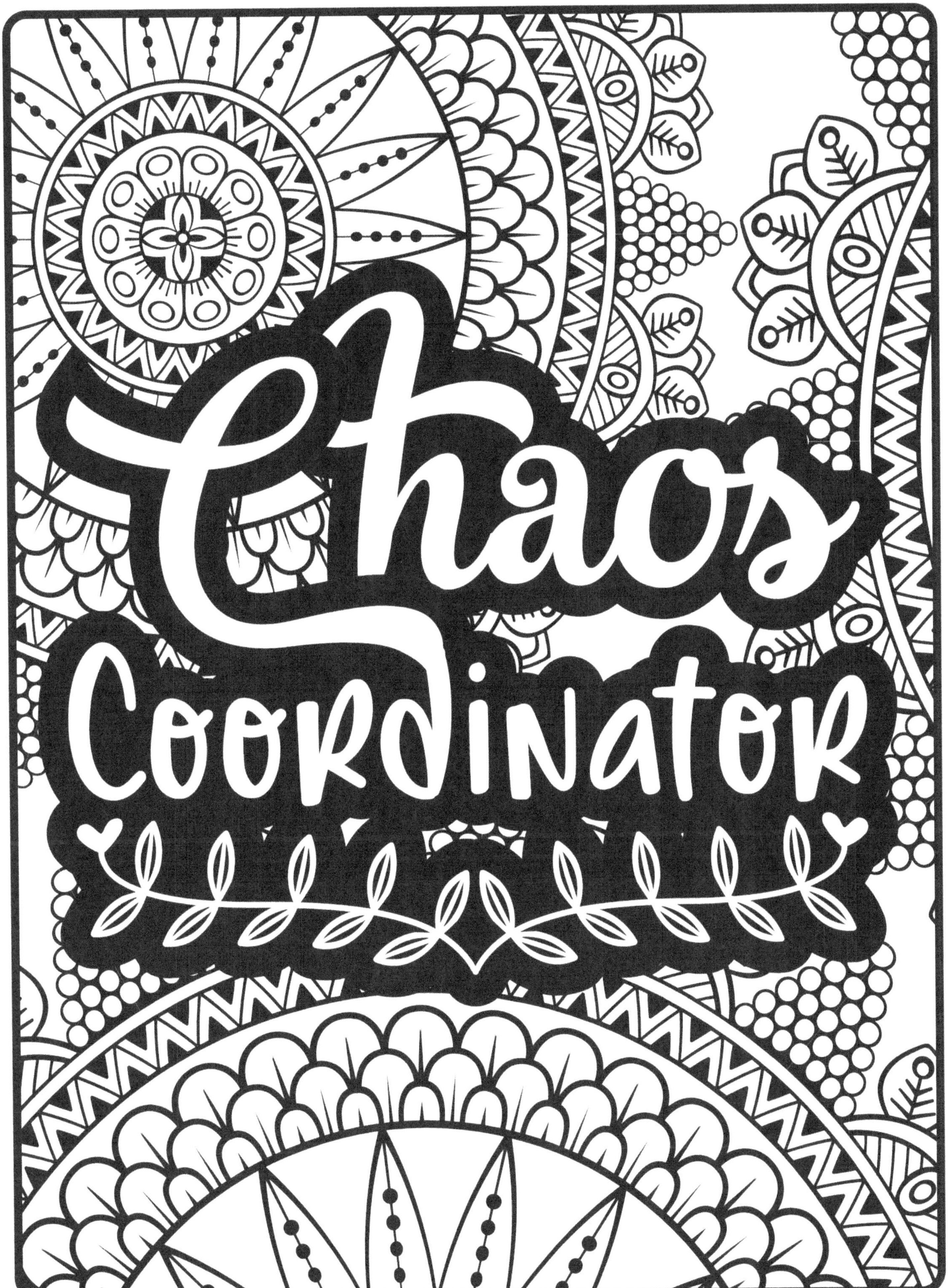
Chaos
Coordinator

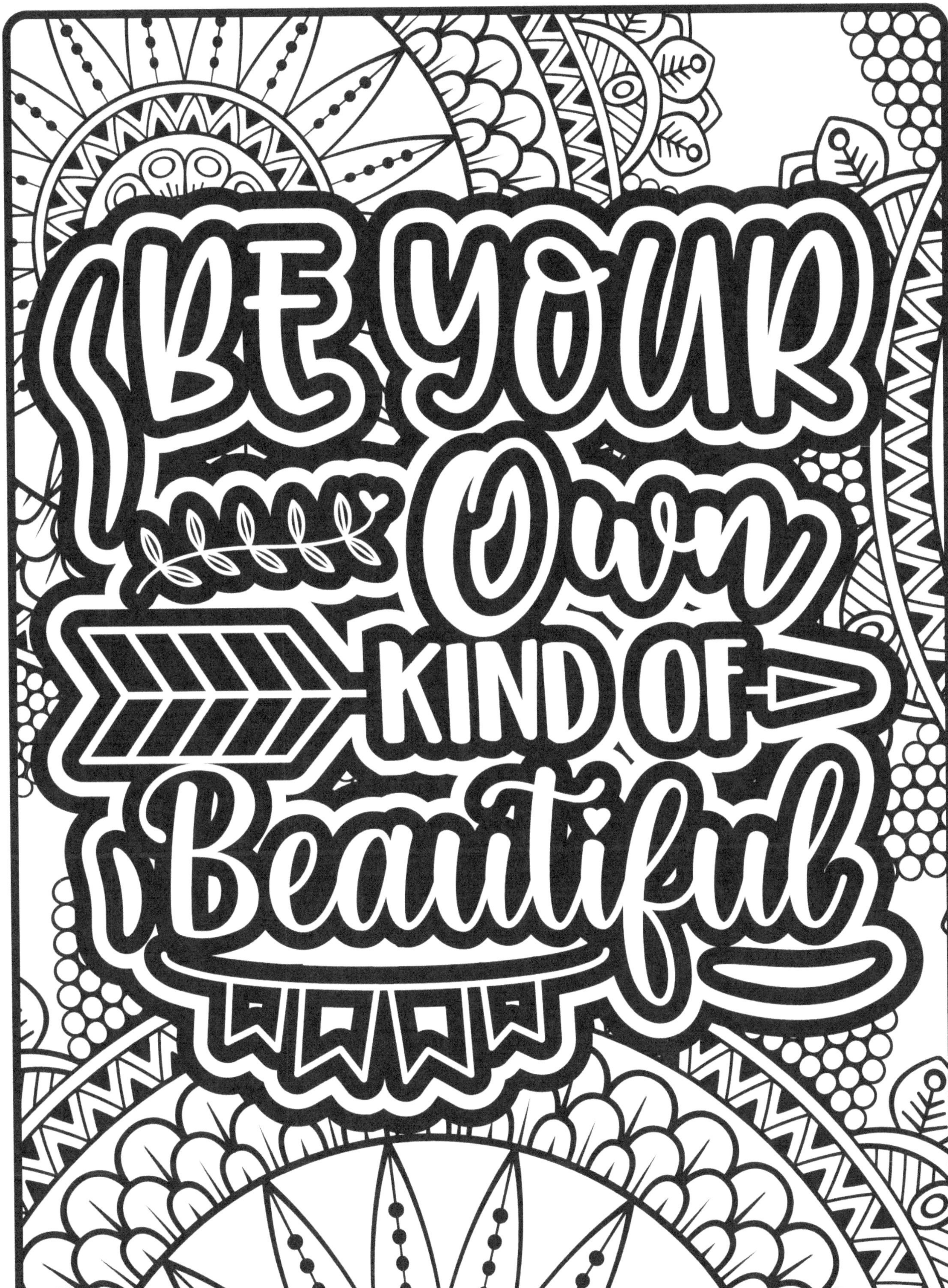
BE YOUR
Own
KIND OF
Beautiful

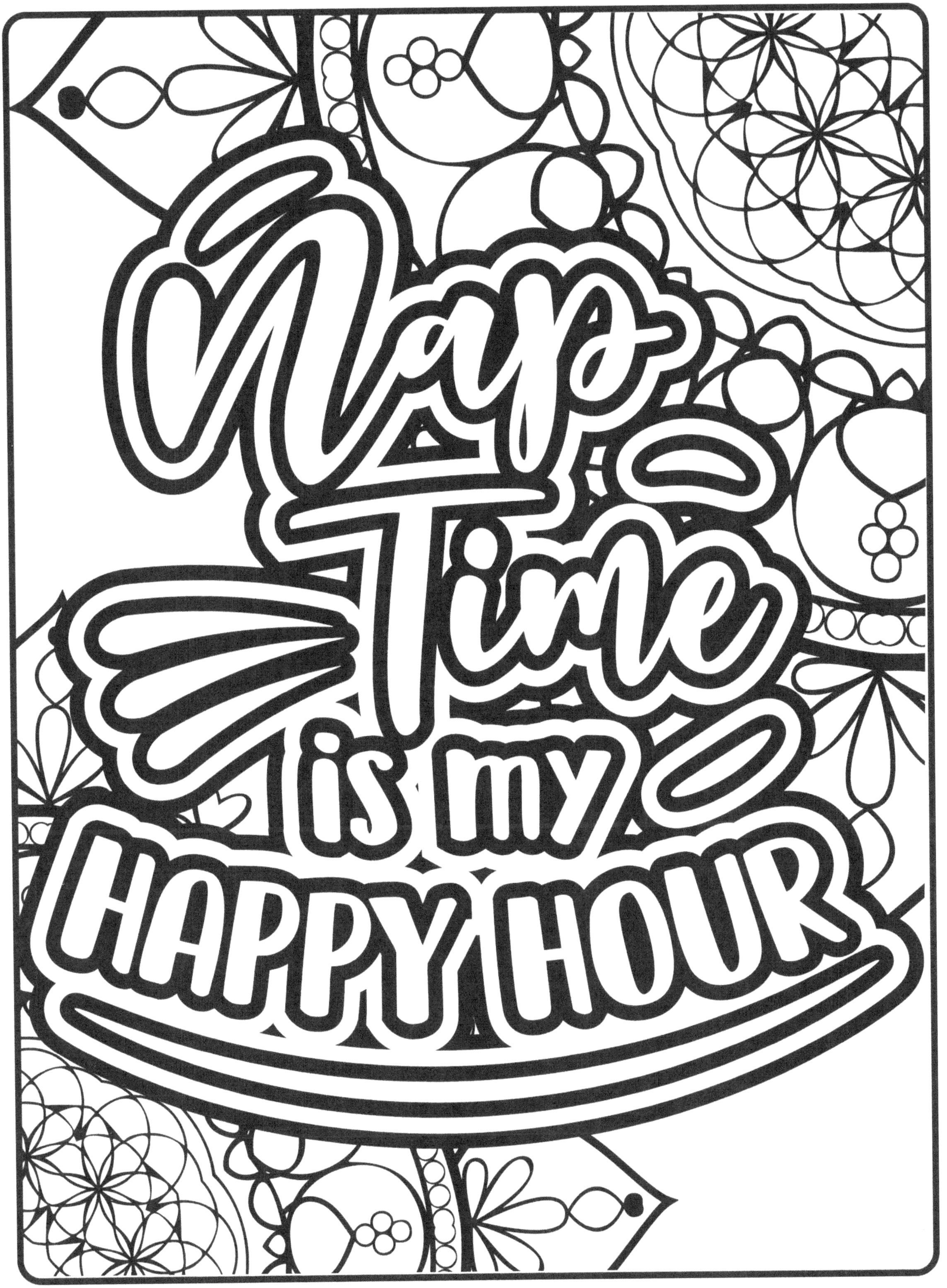
Nap
Time
is my
HAPPY HOUR

www.ingramcontent.com/pod-product-compliance
Lightning Source LLC
Chambersburg PA
CBHW081102240526
45465CB00026B/3221
9798849449067